Writing Effective Business Letters, Memos, Proposals, & Reports

Samuel A. Cypert

Contemporary Books, Inc.
chicago

Library of Congress Cataloging in Publication Data

Cypert, Samuel A.
  Writing effective business letters, memos,
proposals, and reports.

  Includes index.
  1. Commercial correspondence.   2. Business report
writing.   I. Title.
HF5721.C96   1983   808′.066651021   83-5127
ISBN 0-8092-5605-3
ISBN 0-8092-5604-5 (pbk.)

First Contemporary trade paperback edition 1984

Published by Contemporary Books, Inc.
180 North Michigan Avenue, Chicago, Illinois 60601
Manufactured in the United States of America
Library of Congress Catalog Card Number: 83-5127
International Standard Book Number: 0-8092-5605-3 (cloth)
                                    0-8092-5604-5 (paper)

Published simultaneously in Canada by Beaverbooks, Ltd.
195 Allstate Parkway, Valleywood Business Park
Markham, Ontario L3R 4T8 Canada

Contents

Foreword

The most effective business executives I know are good writers. They may not possess a distinctive style or an ability to create memorable phrases. But what they write always communicates their intent.

It's also true that few business people have a natural gift for writing. Exceptions abound, of course. I know insurance executives who write poetry and a cement company operator who is a highly regarded critic and novelist. But, nevertheless, writing usually comes hard to individuals whose aptitude is in business.

So how did the top executives I mention learn to write? They may have had some good college or extension courses in business writing. Or they may have had a mentor at some point in their climb up the ladder who could say something like, "Look, your memos have too many words chasing too few ideas. Boil 'em down. It takes longer to write short, but you save time later because you don't have to explain what you meant to say."

Whatever their individual learning experiences, the ideas and techniques they had to master are the same. For example, there is no shortcut to good English usage that avoids understanding of the parts of speech and their function. By the same token, however, the fundamentals have to be placed in proper perspective. They are tools to help the writer get the job done right, not ends in themselves. No report writer is likely to have a boss grade him on his sentence structure. This book gives the fundamentals the emphasis they require in clear, objective fashion. It also supplies models of good business writing that could substitute for a lot of firsthand experience. The specific advice is practical and it has that quality of utmost importance to a self-help book—it's easily put to use.

Another important aspect of this book is that the author takes a positive approach to all the problems he discusses. Any writer who approaches his task with a positive attitude will find the job far easier. More important, though, the response to his communications is likely to be much more favorable. The ancient wisdom still holds—if you believe you can learn to write well and that this book will help you, it will.

Robert C. Anderson
Editor, *Success* magazine

Preface

As I was doing research for this book I ran across a quotation about the perils of such endeavors. Attributed to Sir Winston Churchill, it said: "Writing a book is an adventure; to begin with it is a toy and an amusement, then it becomes a master, and then it becomes a tyrant; and the last phase is just as you are about to be reconciled to your servitude—you kill the monster and fling it . . . to the public."

To say that writing a book is a difficult task would be a ridiculous understatement, but amid the pain, I confess, I found much pleasure. I like good business writing, and this project gave me the opportunity to review a great deal of it. I have also seen a lot of writing that isn't so good, as every reader of business communications has, and I'm convinced that the need was never greater to improve communications skills. Yet I have known many potentially fine business writers whose talents have been misdirected.

What is the reason for such misdirection? I am convinced it is uncertainty. In business there are few absolutes, as opposed to formal education situations, in which the answers are often clear-cut and measurable. There are no emphatically right or wrong approaches to interoffice writing, and certainly there is no precise way to measure it. There are, instead, countless ways to approach a project, any number of which may be right.

Writing is a practicing art. The more we write, the faster and better we become at it. And emulating good examples of business writing serves to strengthen both our natural and our learned abilities. To this end I have provided numerous examples of effective memos, letters, proposals, and reports interspersed with guidelines and suggestions for improvement.

My intention was and is to provide a single source of information about how to produce good interoffice communications. Subjects addressed in this book range from proposal strategy and planning to the number of spaces one should leave between paragraphs in a letter. However, I've tried to follow my own advice and weight the quantity of information on each topic according to its relative importance to the whole concept and with respect to other elements of the book. Additionally, I have attempted to arrange it in a logical sequence and in an easy-to-use format.

Examples throughout the book were gathered from such diverse sources as trade associations, large multinational corporations, and privately held small businesses. The goal was to provide the broadest perspective possible, in the hope that this approach will cover almost every business writing problem.

The proof of the pudding, however, as Cervantes said almost four centuries ago, is in the eating. I hope you find this book not only palatable, but helpful, informative, and easy to use. If you do, writing it will have, indeed, been a great adventure.

Acknowledgments

Many people and organizations provided examples and other aid in producing this book. Their assistance made it much more interesting than I could have alone. Some of them are listed below.

ORGANIZATIONS

Chicago Tribune; City of New York; General Motors; Industrial Council of Northwest Chicago; Letraset USA, Inc.; Thomas Marin & Associates; Market Focus; McDonough Company; Peat, Marwick, Mitchell & Co.; Professional Photographers of America, Inc.; Selz, Seabolt and Associates; UAL, Inc.; and The Wright Organization.

INDIVIDUALS

Robert C. Anderson, Robert Becker, Derek Carter, Susan Cubar, Peg Deutchman, John T. Flaherty, Richard C. Fowler, Paul Fullmer, Mary Geiser, Linda Habjan, Frank B. Hermes, Sarah Hoban, June Lavelle, Kevin Leonard, Robert Newton, Lee Radtke, Jr., Lynne Richman, Elliott Rubin, Scott Schwar, Stephen Wertheimer, and Janet Wright.

A special thanks goes to my family, who tolerated my absence during vacations, holidays, and weekends when I was closeted with a typewriter and a stack of reference books; and to my secretary, Denise Marin, who not only typed the manuscript in all its various incarnations but offered good counsel about the content as well.

1

Why Write?

"Language is the most important tool available to man. Man can have no more sophisticated thoughts than he has language to formulate them. If he needs additional words, he must invent them to use as tools for thinking and communicating the new thought."

Glenn Doman

Why write in the first place?

These days that question almost always arises in discussions about writing skills. Ours is an audiovisual society, not a literary one. We watch television, listen to the radio, and talk on the telephone.

As long as what is being said is important, however, writing will be important. We have not yet reached the point where every business transaction can be conducted by telephone or over lunch. Many deals are made verbally but confirmed in writing. A quick letter or memo summarizing the terms and conditions ensures that the interested parties agree and eliminates the possibility of later misunderstandings.

The fact that we are a visually oriented society underscores the need for clear writing and can be used to your advantage. Every adman worth his 15 percent knows that in print ads or direct mail it is a good idea to use more graphics and less copy if the audience is under forty. The generation that learned the alphabet by watching "Sesame Street"[1] responds favorably to good graphics.

A recent survey of business school deans and corporate personnel directors found that "poor writing skills are the most common weakness of executives, even though [writing skills] are more important than proficiency in finance and computer use for most jobs." According to the study, "From the first impression that a job application makes to the exposure written communications get internally to important external communications, writing skills can boost or stop an executive on the way up."[2]

Academia may have identified the problem and may have contributed to it as well. Most writing instruction is concentrated in the study of journalism, public relations, and literature; little emphasis is placed on writing in business courses. And none of the communications disciplines is entirely appropriate for learning business writing. The public relations writer prospers in proportion to his success in making his clients' activities newsworthy; the journalist writes for speed and the convenience of busy readers; the literary scholar aims for thoughtfulness and thoroughness.

English composition students sometimes confuse thoroughness with length and place quantity on an equal footing with quality when the length of the dissertation is specified in the assignment. Two thousand words will never suffice if a 2,500-word composition is assigned. As a result, generation after generation of reluctant scholars stretched the composition by dredging up every quotation that might remotely support the point without regard for the author's preference or prejudice. The issue at hand was quantity.

That attitude became so ingrained that one of our first questions about a writing assignment invariably is "How long should it be?"

Length is certainly important. There are, after all, physical and economic limits to consider. But given an option, brevity is usually better. Today's business readers simply don't have or won't take the time to decipher a complex or indirect message.

Your letters, memos, reports, and proposals must compete for attention with hundreds of other messages your reader is exposed to every day, and the pros have the advantage. With megabucks at stake, publishers and advertisers have scrutinized reader response so closely that they can predict almost exactly how we will react to a given topic or sales promotion effort.

Your audience may be more favorably disposed to your message—you may work for the same company or belong to the same club or organization—but that only improves the odds that your reader will open the envelope. How well you write will determine whether your message is read and acted on or if it is put in the "To Read" file that never is.

One way to help you get your message through the maze is to make it more visually appealing. A word of caution here: television and the movies have breathed life into inanimate objects and made the impossible commonplace. Call it the *Star Wars*[3] syndrome: today's audiences—your readers—are not easily dazzled.

The best way to deal with these challenges is to get to the point quickly, say what you have to say in a manner that is easily understood, and make it easy for your readers to extract key parts of your message. All too often business writers do not write to convey information but to impress others with their knowledge or, worse, to mimic the grandiose style of other pompous writers.

Almost twenty years ago John Fielden published an article in the *Harvard Business Review* entitled "What Do You Mean I Can't Write?" Many of his observations are just as timely today as when the article was first written.

Mr. Fielden placed the ability to communicate at the top of what he called the "promotability ladder." He pointed out that correctness in writing is imperative because, unlike verbal communication, it does not have the benefit of the communicator's gestures or tone of voice to facilitate understanding.[4] Writing must stand alone and will be judged solely on its own merit.

Many journalists believe that because writing ability is a natural extension of thinking ability, careless writing results from careless thinking. Columnist Bob Greene takes this idea a step further. He says that he has trouble trusting anything else about a person who doesn't spell correctly. "If he can't even get the spelling of a word right, then why should I put any faith in his version of events or his opinions? Obviously, he is sloppy in his thinking if he can't even take the trouble to make sure of the words he uses."[5]

In addition to correctness, Mr. Fielden properly identified appropriateness, thought, and readability as important elements of good writing. All these characteristics are central to effective written communication and will be dealt with in detail in succeeding chapters, but the best argument for intelligent, tactful, easy-to-read writing is that it helps you sell your own ideas.

In business today, everyone from the president of the largest multinational corporation to the driver of the pizza delivery van has at least one boss to whom he or she is accountable. Several people are involved in almost every level of decision making, and to make informed decisions they need good information. If a potential customer or your supervisor says, "That sounds like a good idea; summarize it in a letter or a memo to me," you can be sure he is planning to circulate copies of it to others involved in making the decision on your proposal. Make it easy for them. Write your message in a fashion that leads them inescapably to the conclusion that they should buy your idea or your product.

This book helps you identify the elements of good writing and offers some tips and techniques you can put to work immediately to improve your memos, letters, proposals, and reports—and get the results you want.

2
Tools of the Trade

"The difference between the right word and the almost right word is the difference between lightning and the lightning bug."

Mark Twain

Much has been said about choosing the right word for the job, yet all too often writers settle for something that is close to the meaning they wish to convey, or they don't take the time to check the meaning of words they are uncertain about. The result is ambiguity that misleads the readers and wastes their time while they try to determine the intent of the message.

Good editors have learned from experience that most writers tend to make the same mistakes, and almost everyone confuses certain words. In her book *Write Right!*[1] Janet Venolia devotes a chapter to confused and abused words, which she says may be the most helpful section of the book. She lists and defines commonly maligned words like *further* and *farther, advise* and *advice,* and *discreet* and *discrete* in an attempt to help writers avoid those common pitfalls. Scores of other good references are available, and there is no excuse for using the wrong word, except carelessness. Unfortunately, your reader may not be able to determine if you were careless with your facts or with your word selection.

As in any vocation, avocation, or trade, there are certain tools that the knowledgeable user can employ skillfully to make the finished product perform the function for which it is designed. Writing is no exception. Reference books such as the dictionary and thesaurus should always be within easy reach when you are writing, but the best tool you have available is your own sound judgment in your choice and arrangement of the words in your message. The key word is *choice*. The selection of words is left to the discretion of the writer, not the typist or reviewer, and choosing the right word is crucial to getting your message through to your reader.

You may associate this study of the order, arrangement, and proper use of words with unpleasant experiences and exercises in English and grammar courses in school, but a certain amount of knowledge is a must if you intend to write well. A brief review of rules and terms relating to words is included in this chapter, broken down by category for easy reference. The intent is to provide a list of definitions, acceptable uses, and examples that demonstrate the working relationship between the tools of the trade and their users.

NOUNS

A noun is defined as "a word that is the name of a subject of discourse (as a person, animal, plant, place, thing, substance, quality, idea, action, or state)."[2] In short, a noun is the part of the sentence that identifies what you are talking about. The concept is easily understood, and most of us have little trouble with nouns.

Examples of nouns: George Bernard Shaw, semiconductors, conference, Chicago, communism, democracy, spinach.

For more detailed information about nouns or any other parts of speech discussed in this book, refer to the bibliography for titles of useful books.

VERBS

The concept of verbs is as simple as that of nouns. Verbs are the words that denote action. To be precise, "Verbs express an act, occurrence, or mode of being."[3] Despite the simplicity of the concept, verbs are the most abused words in the language. Accordingly, we will devote more space to verbs.

Writers are forever disguising verbs as other parts of speech, particularly as nouns.

Wrong: Through conscientious cost control, management was

able to effect an improvement in the corporation's earnings.

Right: Through conscientious cost control, management improved the corporation's earnings.

Not only does the second example state the idea more directly; it also uses fewer words.

Verbs disguised as nouns are most easily recognized by the addition of a suffix such as *ment,* as in the preceding example, or *tion* as in the next example.

Wrong: After giving careful consideration to your proposal we rejected it.

Right: We considered your proposal and rejected it.

Here are some examples of verbs that business writers frequently disguise as nouns:

Verb	*Noun Form*
suggest	suggestion
direct	direction
acquire	acquisition
verify	verification
revise	revision
allocate	allocation
determine	determination
distribute	distribution
reconcile	reconciliation
produce	production
convert	conversion
adjust	adjustment
agree	agreement

Perhaps because we try to soften the language to avoid offending any potential readers, we sometimes go to such extremes that our business language has become mushy and lifeless. A surefire way to put vitality back into your writing is to use the verbs in their purest form, not in their diluted version.

Because verbs are the real power of the sentence, it is important to understand some of the characteristics of verbs. There are two kinds: transitive and intransitive.

A transitive verb takes an object. *Example:* He hit the ball.

An intransitive verb does not take an object. *Example:* She sat here.

These classifications become important to the writer only when you consider other aspects of verbs such as mood, tense, and voice. Later in this section a chart lists (conjugates) the various uses and configurations of a verb and demonstrates the relationship of each to the others. The knowledge of verbs—if you use it—will help you revitalize your writing very quickly.

Voice

The voice of a verb tells whether a transitive verb takes action (active voice) or is acted on (passive voice). An intransitive verb, since it does not require an object to complete its meaning, does not offer a choice for active or passive voice.

Active voice: The treasurer signed the financial statements and distributed them to shareholders, investment analysts, and the media.

Passive voice: The financial statements were signed and distributed by the treasurer to shareholders, investment analysts, and the media.

It is almost always better to use active voice. Active voice makes sentences livelier, clearer, and more interesting because it affixes the action and lets the reader know directly what is happening. Passive voice only adds to the image of unaffixed responsibility and vagueness that is often associated with large organizations. The only time passive voice should be used is when the receiver of the action is more important than the doer, such as in this quotation by William F. Rickenbacker: "Freedom can be squashed by the tyrant or suffocated by the bureaucrat."[4]

Tense

The tense of the verb tells your reader when the act occurred.
Present: The tellers steal.
Past: The tellers stole.
Future: The tellers will steal.

Mood

Mood is Latin for *mode* and is used to indicate the manner or state (mode) in which the action is conceived. English has three moods: indicative, imperative, and subjunctive.

Indicative mood is used to make a statement or ask a question. *Examples:* We purchased new office equipment. Did you purchase the maintenance agreement?

Imperative mood is used to give a command. *Examples:* Go to the bank. Stop here.

Subjunctive mood is used to express a wish or make a recommendation. *Examples:* I wish I were paid according to my profit contribution. Management recommends that the shareholders do not accept the tender offer and vote "no" on the proxy card.

The table below lists the acceptable forms of the verb *throw* for each of the three moods. The active and passive voice are given for each tense.

Indicative Mood: Throw

Tense	Active Voice	Passive Voice
Present	throw	is thrown
Past	threw	was thrown
Future	will throw	will be thrown
Present Perfect	has/have thrown	has/have thrown
Past Perfect	had thrown	had been thrown
Future Perfect	will have thrown	will have been thrown

Imperative Mood: Throw

Tense	Active Voice	Passive Voice
Present (only)	throw	be thrown

Subjunctive Mood: Throw

Tense	Active Voice	Passive Voice
Present	that I throw	that it be thrown
Past	that I threw	that it was thrown
Present Perfect	that I have thrown	that it has been thrown
Past Perfect	that I had thrown	that it had been thrown

Nouns and verbs are the key parts of a sentence. The other parts of speech generally relate to, clarify, connect, or provide a transition between nouns and verbs. The other parts of speech are discussed briefly on the following pages.

PRONOUNS

Pronouns are noun substitutes and are used in sentences as nouns. *Examples:* He, she, I, it. When pronouns are used in the same sentence as nouns, they should agree in number with the nouns to which they relate. *Joe* wants *his* book. The *drivers* must have *their* certificates validated. *Everyone* had *his* (or *his or her*) dinner.

ADJECTIVES

Adjectives modify, explain, or qualify nouns. *Example:* For Christmas my wife gave me *a narrow, gaudy* tie.

ADVERBS

Adverbs modify verbs, adjectives, and other adverbs. *Examples:* He computed his taxes *carefully. Slowly* she swam the length of the pool.

As these two examples illustrate, adverbs are often identified by the *ly* ending and by the fact that they tell how, where, or when something was done.

CONJUNCTIONS

Words such as *and, or, for, nor,* and *but,* used to connect words and phrases, are called *conjunctions. Example:* Both management *and* the shareholders agreed that a hostile takeover was undesirable, *but* if an acquisition could be arranged that would benefit all parties, it should be considered by the directors.

PREPOSITIONS

A preposition is a word that combines with a noun or pronoun to form a phrase that acts as an adjective or adverb. Words such as *for, with, in, from,* and *on* are common prepositions. *Example:* Beauty is *in* the eye *of* the beholder.

AGREEMENT

Another consideration when selecting just the right word for the job is to make sure that nouns agree in number with verbs and that pronouns agree with their antecedents. Singular subjects take singular verbs; plural subjects take plural verbs. *Examples:* The *tellers* balance *their* cash drawers daily. The *teller* balances *his* cash drawer daily.

It is sometimes difficult to determine agreement of subjects and verbs, particularly when they are separated by other words and phrases:

> *"Loyal and efficient work in a great cause, even though it may not be recognized immediately, ultimately bears fruit."*
>
> Jawaharlal Nehru

In this example the subject *work* takes a singular verb, *bears*. Reduced to its basic elements, the sentence is: Work bears fruit. Isolating the principal elements of the sentence immediately makes it apparent that the subject and verb are in agreement. If, after breaking the sentence down into its smallest parts, you still cannot tell whether the subject and verb are in agreement, read it aloud. If it doesn't sound right, look it up.

If the sentence has a compound subject joined by a conjunction, use a plural verb. *Example:* The governor and his public affairs director were here yesterday to dedicate our new building.

governor and director	were
(compound subject)	(plural verb)

Do not confuse conjunctions with prepositional phrases such as *in addition to* or *as well as*. *Example:* The governor, in addition to his public affairs director, was here yesterday to dedicate our new building.

governor	was
(singular subject)	(singular verb)

POSITIVE WORDS

We have heard it said again and again that there are two ways to say something: a right way and a wrong way. What we do not often discuss is that there is more than one right way.

In writing, as in speaking, being brief and concise is not the same as being curt and tactless. The underlying purpose of any written communication is to get the reader to take some action. You may be trying to convince another department or division to help fund some project that you believe will be mutually beneficial, or you may simply want someone to cover a meeting for you, but in each case the response is likely to be more favorable if you use positive words as a persuasive tool. *Example:* My boss is stubborn and bullheaded, and I am tenacious and firmly principled, which sometimes results in a spirited disagreement about the proper handling of one problem or another.

Areas in business writing that are most sensitive are those that deal with problems, money, or personality traits. When describing one of these, take great pains to use positive words. Here are a few to watch out for:

Positive	Negative
methodical	fanatical
economical	cheap
extravagant	costly
uninformed	ignorant
forceful	overbearing
persevering	dogged
firm	inflexible
colorful	gaudy
frugal	chintzy
problem	disaster
meticulous	nit-picking

SHORT FAMILIAR WORDS

"Short words are best and the old words when short are best of all."

Sir Winston Churchill

Throughout this book great emphasis is placed on keeping the message as simple and easy to read as possible. The reason is plain enough: anyone sufficiently important for you to write to is probably too busy to want any more correspondence. It is up to you, the writer, to get and hold that person's attention. The best way to do so is to make it easy for him to understand what you're writing.

I am not proposing that you cast about for a short word when the subject can be explained only by a long technical-sounding word, but don't do the reverse, either. Don't search your thesaurus for a long word when you already have in mind a short word that will do the job quite adequately. Use (don't utilize) short, familiar words whenever possible.

In business writing it is also a good idea to stay away from trendy words and jargon. Any word that requires a judgment about its meaning may be misinterpreted by your reader, and he will almost always misinterpret it in the direction that you like least. If you must use jargon or an acronym, explain the word in parentheses after the first use. *Example:* At one time more than 25 percent of the debenture (bond) market in the United States was comprised of WPPSS (Washington Public Power Supply Systems) offerings.

Wrong: Our CRT operators can now retrieve information from a variety of data bases to provide executives with sufficient detail about prospective clients in order for them to interface effectively with management.

Right: Computer terminal operators can retrieve information about prospective clients from data stored in the computer to provide executives with detailed information so they can hold knowledgeable discussions with management.

BUILDING STRONG SENTENCES

Strong, positive, familiar, active words are the bricks and mortar for building strong sentences. Each sentence will be only as strong as the words used to construct it.

Let's examine the basic elements of a sentence. In its purest sense a sentence is a group of words that makes a statement, gives a command, or asks a question. One sentence should contain only one idea.

A simple sentence has one subject (noun) and one predicate (verb). *Example:*

My secretary left work early.

A compound sentence has at least two main clauses (groups of related words that have both a subject and a verb and can stand alone). *Example:*

I took a long lunch,
(*main clause*)
and my secretary left work early.
(*main clause*)

A complex sentence has one main clause and one subordinate or dependent clause (a group of related words that cannot stand alone). *Example:*

When I stopped taking long lunches,
(*subordinate clause*)
my secretary stopped leaving work early.
(*main clause*)

A compound complex sentence has at least two main clauses and one or more subordinate clauses. *Example:*

When I stopped taking long lunches,
(*subordinate clause*)
my secretary stopped leaving work early;
(*main clause*)
we now usually finish our assignments on time.
(*main clause*)

One Idea

Naturally you will not be able to reduce a concept to a simple explanation in every situation. Often the subject matter is too complex, and a simplistic approach will only insult your reader. You should, however, limit each sentence to one central idea and the thoughts that relate to it. Using unrelated thoughts in the same sentence makes the construction awkward and jolts the reader.

Wrong: The division has experienced severe cash flow problems, and the warehouse roof needs repairing.

Right: Because of severe cash flow problems experienced by the division, management has been unable to provide proper maintenance of facilities, including repairing the warehouse roof.

Better: Because of the division's severe cash flow problems, management was unable to repair the warehouse roof.

Avoid Confusing Detail

If you have done your job well and gathered a great deal of information to support your position, you may be tempted to use it all to prove your point. Resist. Too much detail will only confuse the reader.

Wrong: We visited the company's facilities from the great Pacific Northwest to the balmy beaches of the sunny South with intermediate stops in the Prairie States and the industrial centers of the Midwest in an attempt to determine the effectiveness of our corporate identification, as it relates to our billboards, signage, railway tank cars, and over-the-road motor freight carriers.

Right: We toured the company's facilities around the country to review the effectiveness of our corporate identification program with emphasis on billboards, signs, railway tank cars, and trucks.

Better: We toured the company's U.S. facilities to review the effectiveness of our corporate identification program.

Keep Construction Parallel

Parallelism is using a grammatical construction to reflect the ideas expressed; parallel thoughts require parallel construction. If the correct form is not used, it may not be possible for the reader to determine if the error is in your logic or your writing.

Wrong: The controller is responsible for the approval of invoices, issuing checks to suppliers, and maintenance of financial records.

Right: The controller is responsible for approving invoices, issuing checks to suppliers, and maintaining financial records.

Better: The controller is responsible for:
- approving invoices,
- issuing checks to suppliers, and
- maintaining financial records.

To keep the construction parallel, each phrase should begin with the same part of speech or the same type of phrase. Don't mix nouns with verbs and phrases with complete sentences.

Wrong: The Personnel Department recommended several changes:

- Giving all hourly employees coffee breaks,
- Payment of overtime for all time over 37 hours per week,
- A better health insurance plan should be purchased.

Right: The Personnel Department recommended:

- Coffee breaks for all hourly employees,
- Overtime for all time over 37 hours per week, and
- Purchase of a better health insurance plan.

To check for parallelism of each phrase, connect each one to the introductory phrase. Each should form a complete sentence. In the example above the test would be "The Personnel Department recommended coffee breaks for all hourly employees," and so on.

Keep Modifiers Close to Words They Modify

Words and phrases that are used to describe, explain, or qualify other words in a sentence are said to modify those words. In sentences modifiers should be placed close to the words they modify to avoid ambiguity or changes in meaning. This is particularly important with words such as *only, every, nearly,* and *almost.* Changing their position in the sentence usually changes the meaning of the sentence. *Example:*

Almost everyone invited attended the meeting.
Everyone invited almost attended the meeting.
Everyone almost invited attended the meeting.

Unclear: We purchased patent rights to a line of improved adhesives from International Widgets, Inc., which markets them under the trade name "Fastix" for $12 million.

Clear: For $12 million we purchased patent rights to a line of improved adhesives from International Widgets, Inc., which markets them under the trade name "Fastix."

Optional: For $12 million we purchased from International Widgets, Inc., patent rights to a line of improved adhesives marketed under the trade name "Fastix."

When a modifier is misplaced in relation to the word it is to modify, it may be said to dangle. Usually, however, dangling modifiers are described as modifiers that do not have a word to modify (something missing) or those in which it is unclear which word the phrase is to modify. The Marx Brothers made a hilarious scene from many English teachers' favorite dangling participle: I shot an elephant in my pajamas. The sentence construction when modifiers dangle is often humorous, always awkward.

Wrong: The missing report was discovered by the sales manager after returning from three weeks' vacation in his briefcase.

Right: The sales manager discovered the missing report in his briefcase after returning from three weeks' vacation.

Better: The sales manager found the missing report in his briefcase, where it had been during his three weeks' vacation.

Transition between Ideas

Some words function especially well as bridges between ideas and help provide a smooth, pleasant transition from one idea or one sentence to the next. Examples of good transition words include *also, however, whereas, therefore, besides, accordingly,* and *nevertheless.* Phrases such as *in addition to, in conclusion,* and *as a result* also help guide the reader in the direction you would like him to go. *Example* (transition words and phrases are italicized):

Our investigation revealed that the twenty-ninth floor receptionist had neglected to check the telephone answering machine on Thursday. *As a result,* I did not receive the message that the purchasing agent from our best customer had called. Because I seemingly ignored his urgent message, he gave the order to our competitor. *Nevertheless,* I believe it was an honest mistake, and this situation identifies a weakness in the system: only one person is responsible for checking messages for the executive on each floor. *Accordingly,* I have requested that the office manager instruct his secretary to verify every day that all receptionists have checked their answering machines. *Of course,* this will not rectify the mistake that caused us to lose a large order, but it will ensure that it does not happen again.

Sentence Length

Any discussion about sentence construction almost always includes a reference to sentence length. There is no single optimum length for every sentence. The most effective paragraphs use a variety of sentence constructions and lengths to keep the reader interested. Advertising copywriters have used short staccato sentences in print advertisement to such extremes that our senses have been dulled to a very good attention-getting technique. However, short sentences mixed with long complicated ones provide relief and encourage the reader to read on. *Example:*

I simultaneously ran out of typewriter ribbon, typing paper, and ideas. After a quick visit to the stationery store and a leisurely browse through the reference section of the library, I returned to work. I sat down at my typewriter. I wrote. The result was one of the best feature articles I have ever written.

3

Before Pen Touches Paper

"The creative process requires more than reason. Most original thinking isn't even verbal. It requires 'a groping experimentation with ideas, governed by intuitive hunches and inspired by the unconscious.' The majority of business [people] are incapable of original thinking, because they are unable to escape from the tyranny of reason. Their imaginations are blocked."

David Mackenzie Ogilvy

Much has been made of the so-called creative process. All writers have some method for inspiring themselves to do better work, whether they are writing plays or memos. Each method is probably as individual as the writer, but there are some general techniques anyone can use to make the process less laborious.

Some professions or careers are considered more "creative" than others. Artists, writers, and photographers, for example, are in the business of generating new ideas or new approaches to mundane topics that do require a great deal of originality and creativity. In business, however, the need for creativity has never been greater. Our economy is so complex that even the experts have difficulty understanding it, and it is practically impossible for them to explain it in terms that laymen can understand. Technology is advancing so rapidly that things seem to change before we understand them fully, and we have to learn all over

19

again. Writing about such topics so that readers comprehend is a challenge of some dimension.

That challenge is not limited to highly technical fields. Every aspect of business has its own peculiarities and a corresponding need for creativity when writing about the problems and opportunities associated with it. Don't hesitate to apply to your business writing every ounce of creativity you can muster. Difficult problems require imaginative solutions.

The first step in the creative process is to make sure you have a clear and thorough understanding of what you are writing about. If you try to fake it by using a few buzz words and a lot of technical language, your reader either will see through your ruse or will be unable to understand what you are trying to say. In either event you have failed as a communicator.

In the information-gathering process, make copies of pertinent articles and other published works, take notes in meetings and interviews, and jot down the substance of important telephone conversations. Then, when it is time to write, the creative process will consist of reviewing your notes, organizing the material (and your thoughts) in a logical sequence, and beginning to write.

Depending on the length and complexity of your message, you may need more organization time to plan and develop an outline to follow when you actually begin to write. (See Chapter 4 for outlining assistance.) If the composition is short, such as a memo or letter instead of an outline, make a list of the points you wish to cover in the correspondence, arrange the list in the order in which you plan to present the items, then review the finished piece to make sure you have not omitted anything.

AUDIENCE ANALYSIS

Most business writers have a good general idea about the audience to whom they are writing. It may be the board of directors, an immediate supervisor, or a valued customer, all of whom are important. No matter how familiar you are with your audience, before you write a word it is a good idea to review your audience's characteristics and your reasons for writing.

A clever advertising campaign or gimmick may not be nearly as important as understanding how the audience will respond to the idea. That is the reason for doing extensive testing before committing large amounts of money to advertising in the mass media. There is a good lesson for business communicators in that concept.

Before you write, ask yourself these questions:

- Who is my reader?
- What is his position in the company?
- What is his background?
- Does he have any obvious biases or prejudices that should be avoided?
- If so, what are they?
- Is he expecting this correspondence, or will it be a surprise?
- What is his likely reaction?
- Should the emphasis be on
    how it is written?
    how the conclusions were reached?
    cost/benefit relationships?
    implementation?
    scheduling?
- Consequences of the action?
- Documentation?
- What do I want my reader to do after reading my message?
- Is my reader an influencer or the final decision maker?
- Does he make decisions unilaterally or prefer the counsel of others before making a commitment?
- What is the purpose of my message?
    to inform?
    to stimulate action?
    to document a verbal agreement?
- Is the reader's age, education, experience, sex, or income level likely to be an influence?
- Who should receive copies of the document, and will the fact that certain people have been included on the copy list influence the recipient?
- Will those on the copy list discuss the message with the recipient?
- Are there any hidden audiences?

All of these considerations can affect the presentation of your message and may influence the style and tone of your writing as well. In *The Business Writing Handbook*, author William C. Paxson separates audiences into three categories: general public, expert-laymen, and decision makers.[1] He points out that at various times each of us may be one or the other. We are all expert in at least one field, and we are laymen, decision makers, and members of the general public at times. Naturally, if you are writing about a complicated subject to an expert audience, you handle it differently than if you are writing for the general public.

Occasionally you will be placed in a situation in which you are purportedly writing to one particular reader when in actuality the message is intended for someone on the copy list or someone to whom you plan to send a blind copy. This situation obviously requires more thought and diplomacy. If, for example, you are writing to a plant manager to comment on the disrepair of his facility and sending a copy to the general manager of the division, the chances are good that your reader is not going to respond favorably. How do you deal with such a situation?

Remember, almost everyone hates surprises, particularly nasty ones. Before you issue the report or memo, talk to the plant manager and tell him what you plan to do. You may learn something. He may have instructions to eliminate nonessential repairs until profits improve, or he may have the painters scheduled to come in next week. Even if the worst is true, and he is simply a poor manager and motivator or a plain slob, if he knows in advance that you are planning to write a negative report, he won't be so hostile when he receives it.

Internal auditors are continually faced with problems of this nature. They are chartered by the chief financial officer or the audit committee of the board of directors to review the books and physical facilities of various operating units of the company and to report their findings. The better internal audit departments have developed a good system for dealing with the problem. At the conclusion of the audit they verbally review the findings with the appropriate manager, then later allow him to review a draft of the report and add his comments to the final published version.

Since most interoffice communication deals with finite, easily identifiable primary, secondary, and hidden audiences, it is possible to target the message much more precisely than if you were writing for the general public. By pausing to define the audience before beginning to write, you can focus your efforts on producing a document that relates directly to your readers.

RESEARCH

The Swiss-born American naturalist Louis Agassiz once said, "Every great scientific truth goes through three stages. First, people say it conflicts with the Bible. Next, they say it has been discovered before. Lastly, they say they always believed it."

The purpose of research is to convince readers that the concept is valid or to bring them around to your way of thinking.

Most people have an innate resistance to new ideas or approaches and require some persuasion to adopt another view or to behave differently than before. Businesspeople are more accustomed to change and problems, but they may need reassurance that they are making the right decision. By gathering supporting information and presenting it in a persuasive fashion, you can convince your reader. The amount of research necessary will depend on several factors:

- your knowledge of the subject;
- the complexity of the subject;
- your reader's knowledge of the subject;
- the length of the finished document;
- the number and type of appendices required; and
- the final distribution of the document.

If you are preparing a long report on a technical topic that is going to be distributed to an audience that is unfamiliar with the subject, for example, you may wish to check several sources of information and include an appendix of related information.

The American Marketing Association defines marketing research as "the systematic gathering, recording, and analyzing of data" about marketing problems. Marketing research professionals classify research according to its source of origin. There are two types: secondary (published information), and primary (information acquired directly from the source).

As a business writer you may wish merely to supplement your own knowledge with secondary research gathered from your firm's library or the public library, from government publications, from articles published in trade papers and magazines, or from statistical studies compiled by trade associations. Commercially available computer data bases also provide extensive information, and many firms subscribe to a regularly updated data base that can be accessed by a video display terminal connected through telephone lines to the storage computer.

The Writer's Resource Guide[2] provides a detailed listing of commercially available data bases as well as several other sources of secondary information. Among these are clipping services, colleges and universities, libraries, the government, industrial and commercial firms, and organizations and associations.

Clipping Services

Your company's public relations agency or department probably subscribes to at least one national clipping service that monitors the effectiveness of publicity and perhaps another one (or two) that reads trade publications in your firm's areas of interest. Additionally, many companies subscribe to a computerized service that provides a summary of publications that have written about your firm.

Clipping services usually charge a monthly fee plus a clipping charge for each article cut out. Photocopies or the actual clippings are provided to the subscriber on a weekly or monthly basis.

One limitation of clipping services and the computerized summaries is that readers employed by the services to scan newspapers and periodicals are usually given a name or key word to watch for. Unless specifically instructed, they will not clip related concepts or ideas. Most clipping services, however, are surprisingly thorough and may be a valuable secondary research source.

For prices and information about clipping services you should contact the various bureaus. Three national clipping bureaus (services) and one international bureau are listed below.

Bacon's
14 E. Jackson Blvd.
Chicago, IL 60604
(312) 922-8419

Burelle Press Clipping Bureau
75 E. Northfield
Livingston, NJ 06039
(201) 922-6600

International Press
   Clipping Bureau, Inc.
5 Beekman St.
New York, NY 10038
(212) 267-5450

Luce Press Clippings, Inc.
420 Lexington Ave.
New York, NY 10017
(800) 528-8226

Colleges and Universities

When trying to get information from any large organization, be prepared to bounce around a bit before finally reaching the right person. Despite the fact that they are in the knowledge business, colleges and universities are no exception. Most are cooperative, however, and are willing to provide available information. If you are not sure which department you should be speaking to, try public relations or public affairs first. If the people in that department do not have the information you seek, they can usually steer you in the right direction. The larger universities usually can provide a vast store of information, accumulated through research projects and their own publishing endeavors, if you can find the right source.

Libraries

In business today the gathering, classification, storage, and retrieval of information involves thousands of people and millions of dollars. Most large companies, many professional societies and trade organizations, and most municipalities maintain libraries. The wealth of information available from each is often supplemented by an exchange service among the groups.

The best place to begin looking for information is your own corporate library. Many are well stocked with publications and technical literature pertinent to your line of business and have a librarian whose full-time job is to keep the library stocked with current information, to provide advice or assistance with research, and to help with the operation of microfilm, microfiche, or computer terminals that retrieve the information.

I once wrote a series of nostalgic radio spots about a large multinational company that the advertising department initially would not approve for release. In fact, they questioned the authenticity of my message. The entire department was surprised to learn that I had gotten the information from the firm's own library and that it had been published years ago by one of its own employees.

It is probably a safe bet that most libraries contain more information about more topics than any of us imagine. Consult the library's card index for specific areas of interest, refer to books about how to use the library, and talk to the librarian. Many public libraries even have someone assigned to answer telephone inquiries who can help you determine what is available about a subject or quickly verify a fact for you.

The Government

If you thought you were bounced around when you telephoned your favorite university, try the government. The odds of getting the right person in the right department at the right location on the first try are about the same as winning a million dollars with your first quarter in a slot machine.

Despite being frequently maligned by the public and the media, however, most "bureaucrats" are willing to help if they can. They receive a seemingly endless stream of instructions and requests, which no doubt adversely affects their attitude toward the public. A little tact goes a long way when asking something of a beleaguered public service employee. It is a good idea to have a firm fix on the kind and quantity of information you want before initiating the first phone call; most people don't have the time to chat with you about your project and how you intend to approach it.

If you are not sure where to begin when dealing with the government, write to the Federal Information Center (601 E. 12th St., Kansas City, MO 64106) for a referral to the appropriate agency or contact your local congressman.

To get an idea of the kinds of publications distributed by the federal government, ask the U.S. Government Printing Office (Washington, DC 20402) to place you on its mailing list to receive *Selected U.S. Government Publications.* This monthly catalog lists and describes recently issued publications that are available at a nominal fee or no charge.

Industrial and Commercial Firms

While most companies won't provide information that is confidential or proprietary, many will provide shareholders with copies of annual reports that often describe lines of business, the markets served, and management's review of operations and always include (in publicly held companies) the firm's most recent financial statements. For more detailed financial information, refer to the company's Form 10-K, which publicly held companies must file with the Securities and Exchange Commission. These documents may be provided to shareholders upon written request at no charge; others may be asked to pay a modest fee to cover production costs.

Copies of marketing brochures or information contained in advertising campaigns may be useful in helping you understand a company, its markets, and its management style. Such publications are usually available through the advertising, public relations, or public affairs department of the company.

Professional Societies and Trade Associations

There is a trade association, professional society, or support group for just about everything. *Gale's Directory of Associations* lists hundreds of associations specializing in everything from motion pictures to packing pickles. Many of these groups have a research division that deals specifically with the industry or profession and can make available copies of abstracts, speeches, or articles.

Some serve as a focal point for the collection of industry statistics, which are summarized and distributed to members and others interested in the field. The status of associations was elevated by the consumerism movement and the association's representation of the industry to the media and consumer activists. As a result, many societies now have a consumer affairs representative who can be a valuable resource for information about the industry, and associations are usually very public relations-minded and eager to cooperate. Like government employees, however, association executives are a small group dealing with large numbers of people. Be tactful, and specific and, above all, don't waste their time.

Associations and societies often maintain resource libraries that house published works of their members and other industry leaders, a complete set of association publications since its inception, and other publications associated with the profession or industry. Many maintain biographical files about those who have distinguished themselves in that particular field of endeavor.

If you would like to compare your company's operating ratios or market share with others in the industry, for example, a trade association might be a good place to begin gathering such information.

Electronic Data Bases

With the technological advances made in recent years it is now possible to have vast stores of information literally at your fingertips. Computerized storage and retrieval also permit quick and efficient sorting of the information, making it easy to find exactly what you want.

Some of the more popular data bases are listed below.

The New York Times On Line. This source provides the full text of all *New York Times* articles, or you can request abstracts (briefs) and descriptions of all illustrative material. The service also provides subject indexing. As of May 1982 more than 125,000 items were included, with about 1,800 new items being added per week.

Information is available from:

New York Times Information Service
Mount Pleasant Office Park
1719-A Rte. 10
Parsippany, NJ 07054
(201) 539-5850

The Information Bank. Information about current affairs and business, economic, and political information, as reported in the Final Late City Edition of *The New York Times* and more than 55 other newspapers and periodicals, is provided by The Information Bank. Informative abstracts are available about more than 1 million items (as of May 1982), with more than 2,500 items being added weekly.

Information is available from *The New York Times* Information Service at the address on page 28.

Nexis. Banking and finance and the management sciences are the emphases of this data base. The scope of the service is published material worldwide—newspapers since 1977 and magazines since 1975.

As of April 1982 more than 4½ million characters of information were available. Information about the service is available from:

> Mead Data Center
> 200 Park Ave.
> New York, NY 10166
> (212) 883-8560

DIALOG SDI (Selective Dissemination of Information) Service. The DIALOG data bases offer coverage in science, technology, engineering, social sciences, business, and economics. All data bases, according to its vendor, Lockheed Missiles & Space Company, Inc., are updated regularly.

SDI service is available for 44 data bases, many of them exclusive. For information contact:

> DIALOG Information Services, Inc.
> Marketing Department
> 3460 Hillview Ave.
> Palo Alto, CA 94304

DISCLOSURE II. This service provides extracts of reports filed with the U.S. Securities and Exchange Commission by 8,500 publicly owned companies. Included are extracts of the 10-K and 10-Q financial reports, 8-K reports of unscheduled material events of corporate changes, 20-F financial reports, proxy statements, management discussion, and registration reports of new registrants.

Information about the service is available from:

> Disclosure Incorporated
> 120 Broadway, Suite 1502
> New York, NY 10271
> (212) 732-5964

STANDARD & POOR'S NEWS. The equivalent of the printed *Standard & Poor's Corporation Records Daily News and Cumulative News,* this service offers both general news and financial information on more than 9,000 publicly owned U.S. companies, covering interim earnings, management changes, contract awards, mergers, acquisitions, bond descriptions, and corporate background, including subsidiaries, litigation, and officers.
For information, contact:

Standard & Poor's Corporation
Compmark Data Center
25 Broadway
New York, NY 10004

These are just a few of the scores of data bases available from government and private industry about a wide range of specialized and general topics. A catalog of data bases is available from:

Datapro Directory of On-Line Services
Datapro Research Corporation
1805 Underwood Blvd.
Delran, NJ 08075
(609) 764-0100

Marketing research professionals generally agree, however, that secondary sources of information alone are insufficient. By the time the information is published it may be out of date, or the information available may not be specific enough for your particular need. Hence the need for primary research. Primary sources of information may include your company's own records, your salesmen, dealers, and prospective dealers, your competitors and others in business and the users and potential users of the product.[3]

Company Records

Almost without exception, the first places you should check for information are your company's files and financial reports. After you have reviewed the information that you have, check your firm's personnel directory for others who might be good sources.

Ask them to forward pertinent information to you for review, and ask if you may call back for follow-up information after you have reviewed the material. The same people may be ideal candidates to interview later.

Interviews

Knowing sources of primary information is important, but getting the information may be more difficult. Every company has a resident genius who has vast amounts of information stored "in his head." The only way to extract what you need is to sit down with that person and ask questions. Some tips:

1. Review the material beforehand so you are familiar with the topic and up-to-date on it.
2. Ask the subject of your interview how much time you have.
3. Make a list of key questions. Separate them into "nice to know" and "need to know" categories; ask the need to know questions first.
4. Take notes or make a tape recording of the interview. If you use a tape recorder, remember that it will take you about three times as long to transcribe the tape as the actual interview lasted.
5. Ask for supporting documentation to ensure accuracy.
6. Request that your interviewee review a draft of the section of the document that includes the information he has provided.

Telephone Interviews

It is even more important to be organized and well prepared when interviewing someone on the telephone than in a face-to-face meeting. When a coworker schedules an appointment with you he expects that it will take a certain amount of time. Telephone conversations, on the other hand, are usually shorter. Get to the point quickly and limit the number of questions you plan to ask. For reliable advice about conducting effective telephone conversations, consult your local telephone company. Most publish brochures about telephone etiquette that are distributed free of charge.

Observation

Some things naturally lend themselves to observation as a means of information gathering, such as the traffic patterns around a prospective shopping center site, while others may be limited to observation out of necessity. Your competitors, for example, are likely to be understandably reluctant to divulge information that might help you take business from them, and your only source of primary research may be to observe their businesses from a distance.

Retailers are forever attempting to determine customer habits and impulses and often station researchers at strategic locations to observe and record trends and patterns of behavior. If you borrow from this discipline as a means of gathering information, make sure you understand its limitations as well as its benefits. Statistical sampling requires a certain level of participation before accurate conclusions can be drawn.

A more informal type of observation might be a visit to or a tour of an office or manufacturing facility. This may serve to give the viewer a general impression but should not be used alone as a foundation for making important decisions.

Questionnaires

Some research professionals have elevated questionnaire design almost to an art form and spend hours perfecting questionnaires. In the high-stakes world of marketing, questionnaire design in surveys is all-important. If you are simply trying to get some needed information to complete a report, your procedures need not be as elaborate. There are some things you can do to help your questionnaire succeed:

1. Be brief; your reader probably won't take the time to fill out a lengthy questionnaire. If you limit it to ten questions, your reader may answer them right away instead of setting the questionnaire aside to look at later.
2. Keep the questions simple. An ambiguous question will result in an inconclusive answer.
3. Make the questions easy to answer. Use yes or no or multiple choice formats whenever possible.
4. Make sure the questionnaire is neat. Typeset or typewrite

your questions and make sure there are no mistakes or misspelled words.

5. Allow plenty of space for your reader to write. If the question lends itself to commentary, provide space for it.
6. Give precise instructions. Don't keep your reader guessing about what you want to know.
7. Tell the reader what the purpose of your survey is and to whom the results will be distributed.
8. Offer to send respondents a copy of the summarized information so each can see how his answers compare with others. (Be sure you do; you may need more information later.)
9. Test the questionnaire on a small group to identify any potential areas of misunderstanding. Ask your test group to take a critical look at the questionnaire and offer suggestions for improvements.
10. Print enough copies of the questionnaire for two mailings; send "second request" mailings to nonrespondents.

Independent Advice

Long before "tooling up" the factories and launching an expensive advertising campaign most companies test market new products in areas that reflect the demographic characteristics of potential users. You can duplicate that strategy by testing your idea, concept, or suggestion on others whose opinions you respect before distributing the final document. Circulate your report in draft form to others in your division or department, asking for comments and suggestions both about the information and the way it is presented. Don't merely learn to accept constructive criticism—learn to solicit it actively.

In any form of research, whether it is primary or secondary, always accumulate more information than you can possibly use. Plan to throw out more than you keep, and you might have enough to be highly selective and use only the strongest, best-documented, most persuasive information. For your writing to have substance you must hack away at it until only the essence is left. Only then can you convey the information effectively to others.

4

Getting Down to Business

"Say all you have to say in the fewest possible words, or the reader will be sure to skip them; and in the plainest possible words, or he will certainly misunderstand them."

John Ruskin

There is no right answer to the question "How long should it be?" Yet the question always comes up in conversations about writing. Newspaper, magazine, and book publishers usually pay free-lance writers based on the number of words in the composition, and writers of business correspondence and reports must consider the amount of time the audience might be willing to spend reading the material.

Perhaps the best advice about length is attributed to Tryon Edwards, the late clergyman and author. He said: "Have something to say; say it, and stop when you're done."

With the state of technology today, and the sophisticated equipment available for the storage of information, we have practically reached the saturation point. There is more information available about more topics than ever before. Readers are now more impressed with your taking time to condense and organize the information than with your assembling larger quantities of it.

It is difficult to be brief, and short compositions are often more difficult and time consuming to write than longer ones. All too frequently even the most experienced writers don't allow enough time to do the job right.

The amount of time you should allocate will depend on your familiarity with the subject, its complexity, and the audience's knowledge about the topic. Reducing a highly technical subject to layman's terms will be considerably more difficult than simply reporting the information. Conversely, if you are thoroughly familiar with the material and are writing to an audience of your peers, the process should be shorter and easier.

Some general guidelines may be of value here. Frederick C. Dyer, in his book *Executive's Guide to Effective Speaking and Writing,*[1] says that, after collecting information from free-lance writers and publishers for several years, he arrived at an average writing production of about one book per person per year and about one page of finished work per day.

His research, he says, is confirmed by Larston Farrar in *Successful Writers and How They Work,* a summary of information about the writing methods of 37 modern writers. They say that on the average they actually write about one to three hours a day and produce around 500 words. That is approximately two to three double-spaced typewritten pages.

Ernest Hemingway is said to have kept a chart showing the daily progress of his writing. Days that followed days when he logged 1,000 or more words were usually blank. He took the day off to go fishing. One passage in his *Green Hills of Africa* includes a sentence that is 424 words in length—about a day's work![2]

Several activities associated with publishing take time. Manuscripts must be edited and reviewed, set in type, proofread, corrected, and checked to see that the corrections were made. The same is true in business writing. Writing the composition originally may take less time than the revisions, retyping, corrections, reproduction, and collating. Be sure you allow enough time for all the others who must handle your report to make their contributions. Your typist will probably not operate at top speed and efficiency if you ask every five minutes or so how the job is coming along.

Plan for plenty of time in preparing to write. It takes time to accumulate information; it takes time to organize it; and it takes time to get yourself in the proper frame of mind to write. To shorten the process, prepare an outline that you plan to follow to produce the final document and break the job down into manageable pieces. When I was planning my approach to writing this book I knew the approximate length the publisher wanted and the amount of time I had to write. I worried about my production and the timing so long that at one point my wife asked: "How many words do you have to write every 15 minutes to meet your deadline?" When I immediately knew the answer I decided I had spent enough time in planning and it was now time to get to writing.

OUTLINING

An outline is the framework on which you plan to build the final document. The beginning of the outlining process may consist of nothing more formal than jotting down ideas that relate to the topic as they occur to you. Alternatively, you may elect to gather all your supporting information before you and carefully go through the material, taking notes throughout.

When you are in the information-gathering stage the order in which the information appears is relatively unimportant. Outlining will help you—even force you—to arrange it in the most meaningful fashion.

As you begin the process of organization, arrange the ideas in the sequence in which you wish to present them. Main headings should encompass concepts. They are reinforced by supporting headings and details. Expand on each section until your outline is made up of complete sentences. Then completing the composition is a matter of filling in the supporting information.

Do not try to outline mentally. It is impossible for most of us to retain enough information to outline without getting confused. Some experts, including Harvard psychologist George A. Miller,[3] believe that we can retain only seven units of information. If you doubt the validity of this concept, test yourself by listing the number of brands of toothpaste you can recall. You have, no doubt, seen millions of dollars worth of commercials that tell you about how this or that brand whitens your teeth or stops cavities, yet most of us have difficulty remembering five or six brand names.

A good method of organizing your material is to use 3″ × 5″

index cards. Write one sentence or idea on each card. Then, when you are ready to make an outline, you can do so by arranging the cards in the order you want. Index cards also allow you to see the entire outline by arranging them on a desktop or on the floor. After you have the cards in order, be sure to number them so you don't have to recreate the outline later.

You may prefer to make your outline on a writing pad. Either method is fine. If the entire outline is on a pad, you may have to rearrange some of the material later as you edit and refine the outline. You may need an entire rewrite, or you may be able to finalize the outline by cutting and pasting sections of the material. Whatever method you use is a good one if it works for you.

Composition and writing instructors and authors generally classify outlines according to the way the information is presented. Most agree on three or four types, though they may give them different names. In *Fundamentals of Good Writing,* Brooks and Warren label them *scratch outlines, topic outlines, sentence outlines,* and *paragraph outlines.*[4]

Scratch Outline

Also referred to by some authors as the *jot outline,* this method consists of jotting down random notes as thoughts occur to you or as information is uncovered during your research. This method is informal, and the information is not usually well organized. The advantage of the jot outline is that you can quickly get ideas down on paper for reference later when you are ready to formalize your outline. You will, of course, have to develop a more complete, better-organized outline before beginning to write the final document. However, the material you have gathered through your scratch outline method will be of great value in building a final outline.

Topic Outline

As the name implies, the topic outline arranges the material according to the subject matter, using key words or sentence fragments as headings and subheadings. This method does require you to organize units of information according to importance and the relationship of each to the other. Headings identify key concepts, and subheads are used to support, quantify, qualify, or elaborate on the main topic. A topic outline is considerably more organized than a jot or scratch outline and may be used as your final blueprint for the finished piece, whether it is a lengthy report, a proposal, or another internal document. For reports issued at regular intervals, such as financial or sales reports, some companies provide preprinted forms for completion by the writer or ask you to follow a set order of presentation. Such guides function as a topic outline to keep the writer organized and condition the recipients of the reports to look for similar information in the same location each reporting period.

Sentence Outline

By the time you have completed a sentence outline you have organized the information in such a final form that writing the composition should be easy. Complete sentences used throughout the outline state complete thoughts, both for heads and subheads, as well as for supporting points. The sentences should be direct and to the point and help you focus on the most important parts of this framework that will guide you to the final document. Generalized sentences and concepts will only cause you difficulty later when you attempt to write, and you will eventually be required to rethink your entire approach and identify the key parts of the message. The more complicated the material, the more complete your outline should be. Keep related ideas together, make sure headings (main topics) don't overlap, make sure the material is arranged logically and that you are properly emphasizing each point or idea. Your finished outline should parallel the finished document not only in the order and logic of presentation but also in the amount of space devoted to each element.

Paragraph Outline

The paragraph outline is not as versatile as topic and sentence outlines. It arranges the material by paragraph, in the order in which it is to be presented in the final document, but it does not provide headings, subheadings, and supporting points used to point the way for the writer in the final composition. Paragraphs generally deal with key topics and may confuse you when you attempt to arrange them in any meaningful order. This form of outline is more useful in short compositions such as memos or letters, but if your finished product is to be a lengthy or complicated report or proposal, the topic or sentence outline is more functional.

It is possible to use a combination of all four to help you force yourself to organize your thoughts and gradually work toward the final document. You may begin, for example, by gathering information at random, jotting key words or thoughts on a note pad in the form of a jot or scratch outline. The next step would be to fashion a topic outline that concentrates on organizing the material in a logical fashion according to key topics. At this point you make a judgment about what should be main headings, subheadings, and supporting points. Next you develop the topics and ideas into complete sentences and finalize the outline, paying particular attention to the amount of space you will devote to each portion. Finally you expand the sentences into paragraphs, using the outline sentences as topic sentences in the paragraphs. To complete the final document all you need do is provide some transition sentences, then edit the complete composition to smooth the flow of words and ideas and to remove any superfluous, redundant, or unnecessary material that you may have included inadvertently.

Whichever method you use, it is a good idea at the beginning to write down a sentence that capsulizes your message or the conclusion that you would like your reader to reach. Then, throughout the outline development, make sure that every point, every idea supports the initial premise.

Outlining Example

As an outlining exercise, let's assume the following scenario. You have been sent by the president of your company to the Newark, New Jersey, plant to determine the likelihood of a strike when the United Rubber Workers contract expires in six months. You are to spend two days on a fact-finding mission, then report your findings and recommendations to your chief executive officer in a memo. Your memo is to be limited to one page.

You spend the time talking to as many of the appropriate

people as possible, jotting your impressions and observations on a note pad. You review your notes upon returning to the office and find that you noted the following:

1. The plant manager seems preoccupied with profit goals of the plant. He has installed several internal financial controls to monitor the effect of cost-cutting measures that he has installed in marketing, administration, and manufacturing.
2. During your interview with the plant manager you asked his opinion about the likelihood of a strike. He does not consider it very likely because:
   • the union has not struck the plant in ten years;
   • the economy is bad, and jobs are scarce;
   • the plant principally makes automotive parts, and the depressed conditions in that industry have caused unions to make unprecedented concessions in contract negotiations.
3. You receive conflicting information from the manager of manufacturing. In confidence he tells you that he sees indications that the rank and file of the union "want to walk." He believes the union leadership has become worried about the loss of status unions have experienced recently and that they are convinced management thinks they have become complacent since they have not struck the company in ten years. He is very worried about a strike.
4. The human resources director senses an air of uneasiness about the contract negotiations. He is an old-timer with the company and seems to have a good sense of what is going on and a balanced perspective about the relations between labor and management.
5. Because of the delicacy of the situation and possible antitrust implications, you have been advised not to speak directly about the contract to the hourly workers or the union management. During plant tours, visits to the lunchroom, and walks around during breaks and at lunchtime, however, you observe the following.
   • There seems to be considerable dissatisfaction among the union members that is more than the usual grousing about work.
   • When the workers find out you are from corporate head-

quarters, they take a few verbal potshots about the way the company treats its employees, and one of the supervisors makes a reference to a safety measure that was not installed on schedule because, he presumes, of cost considerations.

6. A telephone call to the corporate industrial relations manager confirms your apprehensions. His impressions are about the same as yours, and he fears a strike. He reminds you that, once the workers are out, it is impossible to predict the length of a strike and that the union has a substantial strike fund since it has not gone on strike in ten years.

7. Despite the plant manager's reassurances that a strike is unlikely, you are convinced that the odds are more than 50 percent in favor of a strike.

Topic Outline Example

Newark Plant

Likelihood of a Strike

I. Objective

    A. Evaluate likelihood of strike

    B. Report back and make recommendations

II. Information-gathering methods

    A. Interviews

        1. plant manager

        2. manufacturing manager

        3. human resources director

        4. industrial relations manager

    B. Observations

III. Conclusions

    A. Better than 50-percent chance of strike

B. Company should make appropriate preparations

IV. Recommendations

A. Take steps to avoid strike

1. Intensify negotiations to sign contract

2. Address morale problem

a. Hold company meetings

b. Correct safety violations

B. Prepare for strike

1. Do financial evaluation

a. inventory stockpile

b. effect of plant shutdown

2. Purchase strike insurance

Final Memo Example

MEMORANDUM

To: Curtis B. Smith   Date: May 13, 19xx
          President

From: Samuel A. Cypert   cc: Lloyd Dye,
          Industrial Relations   Director
            Department   Industrial
                                      Relations
Subject: Newark Strike Possibility

CONFIDENTIAL

As you requested, I visited the Newark, New Jersey, facility in an attempt to evaluate the likelihood of a strike when the United Rubber Workers contract expires on November 30, 1983.

My conclusions are based on interviews with

several key executives, including the Newark plant
manager, manufacturing manager, human relations
director, and the corporate industrial relations
manager assigned to Newark negotiations. Although
there are conflicting opinions, the majority of
those I interviewed believe a strike is likely.
Based on the information I gathered and my observations at the facility, I believe that there is more
than a 50-percent chance of a strike.

This conclusion is based on the following:

- a general unrest among the hourly
  workers;
- the attitude of union leadership that
  it needs to reestablish itself as a
  dominant force;
- the existence of a large strike fund;
  and
- possible management inattention to
  union problems because of other
  pressing matters.

Although I recognize that these observations
are highly subjective, such is the nature of
industrial relations. Very often management and
labor cannot seem to come to terms because the
issues become emotional, not because of any logical
reasons.

In order to deal effectively with either eventuality I suggest we make every effort to avoid a strike but prepare for the worst. Specific-ally, I recommend:

1. Negotiations should be intensified to encourage signing the new contract before the present one expires.

2. Newark management should immediately correct safety violations and begin holding company meetings to address grievances and improve morale.

3. The financial division should:

   ● develop a financial pro forma based on a strike of 30 days, six months, and one year in duration;

   ● review the financial consequences of stockpiling inventory to prepare for a strike that doesn't materialize; and

   ● investigate the purchase of strike insurance.

4. Marketing should evaluate potential damage to customer relations if the plant is shut down and we are unable to supply our customers.

After the information is assembled and analyzed

by each group, senior representatives from marketing, operations, industrial relations, and finance
should meet to review our options, decide which
course of action to follow, and develop an implementation strategy.

Please let me know if you would like additional
information, or if I can be of further assistance.

Outline Design

The outline generally is organized according to the guidelines
below:

I. } Roman numerals are used for major headings or concepts

A. }
B. } Capital letters are used for subheadings of primary significance

1. } Arabic numbers are used for subheadings that are of lesser (sec-
2. } ondary) significance or to support major headings.

a. } Lowercase letters are used for subheadings of lesser significance
b. } than Arabic numbers or to identify bullet points, numbers, or
other lists.

II. } If you have one Roman numeral, Arabic number, uppercase, or
lowercase letter, you must have at least one more. If you have
only enough information for one heading or subheading, incorporate it into another part of the outline. Never use only one
letter or numeral.

WRITING STYLE

*"Who can confidently say what ignites a certain combi-
nation of words, causing them to explode in the mind?
Who knows why certain notes in music are capable of
stirring the listener deeply, though the same notes
slightly rearranged are impotent?"*

William Strunk, Jr.,
and E. B. White in
The Elements of Style[5]

Writing style is perhaps the most difficult aspect of writing to
explain and certainly the most difficult to achieve. Style is that
aspect of your writing that is uniquely yours, something that sets
you apart from all others. There are some aspects of style—correctness and precision, word choice, and the use of active versus
passive voice, for example—that are relatively easily learned,
while the more subjective aspects elude us. Mark Twain wrote
with a style that was unmistakably his, yet he used simple constructions and never missed an opportunity to advise others to do
the same. Nevertheless, his pithy statements laced with irony and
humor are immediately recognizable as Mark Twain's style.

Every popular writer strives to distinguish himself from the
masses through this elusive component of writing, and so should
business writers. This is not to say that you should attempt to
make everything you write complicated or flowery; nor should
you make it so simple as to insult your reader. Business writing
generally should be pleasant, direct and forthright, succinct and
to the point. If you follow those guidelines, you can be assured
that your writing will be received favorably and, gradually, as you
become more proficient at writing, your educational background,
your native intelligence, your sense of humor, and your personality will subtly influence your style until your friends and associates recognize your writing style as surely as they recognize their
favorite author's style.

The quotation from Strunk and White at the beginning of this
section comes from the chapter on style in their book. If you do
not have a copy of *The Elements of Style,* get one and keep it for
ready reference. It is a classic in the field and has influenced
generations of writers since it was first published in 1919, yet it is
regularly updated to keep the material current.

While it is nice to receive compliments about your writing style, remember that the principal purpose of business writing is to communicate, usually with the intent of persuading your reader to take some form of action. What you say is as important, if not more important, than how you say it. Use the stylistic techniques such as rhythm, sentence structure, diction, metaphors, and harmony[6] to enhance your ability to communicate more effectively.

DICTATION AIDS

No doubt you know someone who can generate page after page of a report and letter after letter with seemingly little effort by dictating his thoughts to his secretary or into a recording device. I am sure there are some who can dictate clearly and in an organized fashion, but I have never met anyone who could consistently produce high-quality writing by dictating. Most of us are too wordy and our thoughts are too disorganized to say it as well as we should. The difficulty of dictation is increased with the complexity of the material. A report that was dictated reads like a report that was dictated.

If you are required to dictate for some reason, there are some techniques that you can employ to improve the quality of the final document:

1. If the finished product is going to be more than a one-page letter or memo, make an outline to follow as you are dictating.
2. For a one-page letter or memo, make a list of things you plan to cover and the order in which you plan to present the information.
3. Allow plenty of time for review and editing. Do not assume it is your typist's responsibility to make sure the language is correct and that there are no mistakes. Final responsibility for the content rests with the writer.
4. Ask your typist to give you a double-spaced draft for review and revision before final typing. Be prepared to cut and paste and otherwise reorganize the material.
5. Spell technical words, names, colloquialisms, and words you have a tendency to mispronounce or pronounce carelessly.

6. Carefully review every draft and the final version. Ask someone else to review important documents. Both you and your typist are too familiar with the material, and you may tend to overlook misspelled words and awkward construction.

7. Don't dictate unless there is no other way to do the work.

5

Editing Your Own Work

"You become a good writer just as you become a good joiner: by planing down your sentences."

Anatole France

A colleague of mine once observed that to be a good editor one needs a strong killer instinct. You have to be ruthless in your search for words, phrases, sentences, paragraphs, and whole sections that can be cut from a piece without damaging the meaning of the original construction.

It is without question more difficult to edit your own work than to edit the work of others. The principal reason for the difficulty is that, as the writer of the material, it is almost impossible to disregard the intent of the message and concentrate exclusively on the grammar, punctuation, spelling, style, and other elements of good construction. It is also difficult—if not totally impossible—to be objective about your own writing. You are simply too close to it to disassociate yourself and become a disinterested reviewer or editor.

There are some things you can do to help edit your own work. *Read it aloud.* Find a quiet place, close the door (so your coworkers won't be annoyed or think you've begun talking to yourself) and read every word aloud. In doing so, your ear forces your mind to operate at a slower speed, and you will catch mistakes that you would have otherwise skipped over. You will also find that this technique helps you identify rough transitions and sentences, errors in grammar, and unclear thoughts. If it sounds wrong, it probably is. Look it up; then fix it.

Let it cool. Allow enough time so that you can set the composition aside and return to it in two or three days. You will be more objective after you have been away from the material for a while. In another day or two, revise the material again to see if you still agree with the changes you made and take one more careful look. Then send it to your typist. After it is typed, review it once more to make sure that there are no misspelled words and that all sentences and transitions are smooth.

Make a list. Most people continually misspell the same words or make the same grammatical errors. You are probably no exception. Keep a list of errors that you usually make, with examples of correct and incorrect usage. This will not only minimize the time you spend checking references, but also help you eventually correct those errors in many cases. Every editor has a list of favorite frequently misused and misspelled words. Here's mine.

accessible	accommodate	advantageous
affect (influence)	among	analysis
apparent	beginning	calendar
carelessness	commitment/committed	conscientious
consensus	consistent	criteria/criterion
definitely	disappear	effect (result)
embarrass	erroneous	exaggerate
familiar	feasibility	fulfill
guarantee	illegible	immediately
independence	indispensable	irresistible
it's (its)	jeopardize	likelihood
labeling	liaison	miscellaneous
maintenance	manageable	necessary
moral (morale)	mortgage	occurrence
noticeable	occasionally	permanent
omitted	parallel	principal/principle
personal/personnel	precede/preceding	recommend
questionnaire	receive	stationary/stationery
refer/referring	separate	tendency
subtle/subtlety	supersede	unanimous
their (there)	thorough	usage
unnecessary	wholly	whether

To rewrite or not to rewrite. Most editors who spend every work day reviewing and correcting the work of others learn to think in a modular fashion. They rearrange the material through the use of editorial marks that serve as cues to typesetters, word processing operators, and typists without having to rewrite the paragraphs. Some cut and paste paragraphs in a difference sequence to facilitate clarity or to present the material in a more logical fashion.

Occasionally, however, it becomes necessary to completely rewrite a section or portion of a composition. The same is true with your own work. If the sentences are convoluted, the transitions choppy, and the organization erratic, your only alternative is to rewrite the offending portion. Your deadline for publication will limit the number of rewrites possible and the amount of time you can realistically spend on revisions. Otherwise, the perfectionists among us might never complete our work. It is safe to assume that in most cases there is always room for improvement, but the key is to be able to determine when "good enough" really is.

FIVE-POINT REVIEW

Short documents with limited distribution and of lesser importance will obviously require less time and attention than lengthy reports and proposals. If the document is important and several pages in length, I suggest a five-point review:

1. Immediately after you have finished writing, edit the document to make sure you're saying what you intend to say; that transitions are smooth, punctuation is correct, spelling is accurate; and that you have not inadvertently left gaps in your writing when you shifted from one topic to another.
2. Allow the report or proposal to cool for two to three days; then take a fresh, objective look at it. Check the same things you did in step 1.
3. Set the document aside once again and return to it in another day or two. Make sure you still agree with the changes you made in step 2.
4. Send it to your typist. When it returns, proofread it and make a final check of the entire composition to make sure it reads well.

5. Have your typist correct any spelling and punctuation errors you noted in step 4. Check to make sure the corrections were made and review the sentence before and after the one in question to be sure another mistake was not made during the correction process.

TYPES OF EDITS

As observed earlier, the length and importance of the document will influence the amount of time you should spend editing the work. A proposal to the board of directors that involves millions of dollars should be given more attention than a short informational memo to others in your department.

The five-point review presented earlier indicates that at various checkpoints in the process you may wish to perform different types of edits, and there may be occasions when there simply is not enough time for a complete and thorough editorial review. These and other factors may influence which of the following types of edits you choose to perform.

Proofreading

As the name implies, proofreading is merely checking the copy to make sure there are no misspelled words, typographical errors, or errors in punctuation. In short, proofreading assures that the final typed document follows your instructions exactly. The proofreader does not make any judgments about the material or suggestions for improvement.

Proofreading is never easy, but it is especially difficult to proofread your own writing. Your mind almost always focuses on the content of the document, not on the spelling and punctuation. To avoid this, try having someone else read the composition to you, or read it aloud yourself, or try reading from the end to the beginning to focus your attention on the words instead of the message.

When you reach tricky words in the text, pause and proofread those words a letter at a time to check the spelling. Keep a dictionary handy to look up words you are unsure about and refer to your list of frequently misspelled words that may look right but are actually spelled wrong.

Cursory Edit

Sometimes referred to as a *perfunctory* or *superficial edit*, this activity denotes a hasty review that at best will identify problem areas in content or logic to be addressed later, as well as attempts to correct spelling, punctuation and grammatical errors.

In a cursory review, whether it is his own or someone else's work, the editor does not take the time to rewrite awkward constructions or spend a great deal of time rearranging sections of the report.

Obviously, a cursory edit is insufficient if the final document is to be distributed to a wide audience or is important enough to be studied at length by a group you wish to influence. In such documents a cursory edit might be performed as a final check before distribution or publication.

In-Depth Review

Performing a review in some depth involves not only the grammatical aspects of editing (including spelling and punctuation) but also logic, construction, transition, and tone of the report, proposal, or other document.

If parts of the composition need some rewriting, this would be done as a part of an in-depth review. Paragraphs and sentences might be rearranged and more precise language substituted in places.

For most documents, an in-depth review, followed by a cursory edit and final proofreading, assures good editorial integrity throughout the composition.

Comprehensive Editorial Review

The difference between an in-depth review and a comprehensive edit is roughly the equivalent of the difference between performing surgery with a scalpel and doing so with a meat cleaver. If you plan to take a comprehensive editorial look at your writing, nothing is sacred. You may wish to hack apart entire sections of a report, to be stitched back together in a different order.

A comprehensive editorial review should be necessary only infrequently or in situations in which the document is so important that every word and every comma should be questioned before final publication. Examples of such documents might be the corporate annual report to shareholders and extensive proposals for large pieces of business when the purchasing decision will be made on the evaluation of the proposal alone.

In an ideal situation, it would be desirable to perform each of the preceding types of edits on every lengthy document you write. Begin with a comprehensive editorial review and end with proofreading the final version. In business, however, there are few ideal situations, and every writer is subject to time constraints and must adjust the amount of time he can devote to any composition according to its rank on the priority ladder.

READABILITY FORMULAS

Although readability is generally regarded as a subjective analysis, some authors have developed mathematical formulas for calculating the level of education your readers must have to understand certain levels of writing and have arrived at a measure of readability. Some of the better-known systems are reviewed here. No formula will provide infallible results but should be used as a guide to help you determine whether you are writing over your readers' heads, being too simplistic, or addressing them directly in a fashion they understand and appreciate.

Fog Index

Perhaps the best known and most often quoted, the Fog Index was developed by Robert Gunning[1] and is used to determine the number of years of education (up to seventeen) the reader must have to understand the writing.

To calculate the Fog Index you need a sample of at least 100 words. Compute it as follows.

1. Determine the average number of words per sentence. Treat independent clauses as separate sentences.
2. Count the number of words with three or more syllables. Do not count capitalized three-syllable words, verbs that have as their third syllable the endings *es* or *ed,* or short words combined to make a longer one (e.g., *manpower*).

3. Add the figures obtained in steps 1 and 2 and multiply by 0.4; round to the nearest whole number. The result is the Fog Index in years of schooling. A fog rating of twelve, for example, assumes that the text could be read and understood by a high school graduate, a sixteen would require readers to have a graduate degree to read and understand the message.

Most mass circulation magazines and newspapers fall into a range of about eight to ten, while *The Wall Street Journal, Fortune,* and other higher-quality publications score a fog rating of about ten to twelve.

Smog Index

A formula similar to Gunning's Fog Index, developed by G. H. McLaughlin,[2] also results in a measure of education necessary to understand the material. McLaughlin's formula, which he called the Smog Index, is calculated as follows.

1. Select ten sentences from the beginning, ten from the middle, and ten from the end of the composition.
2. Count the number of words with three or more syllables, except proper names.
3. Take the square root of that figure and add three.

The result, again, is in number of years of education required to read and understand the text. Either the Fog Index or the Smog Index may be used as a guide to the level of complexity you wish to use, based on your analysis of the audience to which you are writing.

Flesch's Reading Ease Score

This readability formula, developed by Rudolph Flesch,[3] gives a score between 0 (unreadable) and 100 (can be read by anyone). It is calculated using the following method.

1. Count the average number of words per sentence and the average number of syllables per 100 words.

2. Multiply the average sentence length by 1.015.
3. Multiply the number of syllables per 100 words by 0.846.
4. Add the figures resulting from steps 2 and 3 and subtract the sum from 206.835. The result is the Reading Ease Score.

Computerized Readability Formulas

Here again modern technology can aid the writer. Let a computer perform the calculations for you by using the STAR program developed by General Motors.

Originally initiated by the automaker to simplify shop manuals for people who use them, the STAR program was devised by the Service Research Group of GM's Consumer Relations and Service Staff, which collected samples of manuals and found that much of the knowledge they contained was not expressed clearly.

To define the reading problems it found, the group turned to Flesch's reading ease formula, computerized it for easy use, and now makes available on request a copy of the program and a brochure describing it.[4]

According to GM, the STAR program helps clarify "dense" language. By listing words of three syllables or more, the printout makes it easy to remove what they call *hi-cal* words from any writing.

Since most readability formulas use a sample based on an average, none are absolutely precise but all are reliable when used to compare your writing to that of others. Generally, readability formulas encourage using short sentences and simple words. In business writing this is not always possible, particularly when the subject matter is highly technical. Keeping the Fog Index low, however, means that on an average the writing is easily understood despite the difficult passages, and the short, simple words and sentences give your reader a respite from the more laborious reading.

QUICK EDITING TIPS

Count the pieces. Before you begin, make sure that you have all the pages, headings, appendices, charts, and graphs, and that all the pages of the draft are in the proper order. Don't waste time later looking for missing pieces or exhibits or rearranging pages that are out of sequence.

Keep references handy. Always have a good dictionary of recent vintage within easy reach when you are editing anything. Reference books, like most other things, become out of date. Buy new ones every few years. Other "must" references include a thesaurus, your list of your own frequently misused or misspelled words or a good commercially available checklist, your favorite writing and grammar reference, and any technical or medical dictionaries or references that are peculiar to your profession or your company's lines of business.

Check the layout. The visual presentation of your writing is very important when dealing with busy readers. (For some techniques to grab your readers' attention, refer to Chapter 7.) Use a variety of centered and flush left headings, indent the paragraphs, use bullets and numbers to break up the text. Make sure that all titles, subheadings, charts, and graphs appear where they should.

Use parallel structure. As you review the composition, be alert for constructions that are not parallel in logic and in presentation. Frequent problem areas are words used in a series, lists, or bullet points. Title pages, headings, and subheadings should also be parallel in construction.

Make sure subjects and verbs agree. The best check for agreement is to reduce the sentence to its basic elements. Plural nouns take plural verbs, and pronouns should agree in number with their antecedents.

Look for misplaced or dangling modifiers. Make sure modifiers are close to the words they modify and that there are no dependent phrases or clauses with nothing to modify.

Delete unnecessary words. Use as few qualifying or descriptive adjectives as are absolutely essential to get the message across. Don't limit your hit list to long, pompous, or ambiguous words; keep an eye out for words such as *a, an,* and *that,* which can be deleted without affecting the message. Watch for excessive use of transitional words and phrases such as *in addition to, also,* and *accordingly.*

Use an active and personal structure. If you use the passive voice, make it a conscious decision. Use the active form of the verb whenever possible. Write for your reader. Use *you* and *yours* more than you use *I, me, we, ours,* and *mine.*

Correct spelling errors. If you are not sure how a word is spelled, look it up. Your reader won't attach much importance to the composition if it is filled with errors.

Follow a consistent editorial style. If you always capitalize some words or use certain abbreviations such as when referring to your firm, use the same style throughout. If you do not have a corporate editorial style manual, use the U.S. Government Printing Office's *Style Manual,*[5] The University of Chicago Press's *A Manual of Style,*[6] or Prentice-Hall's *Words into Type.*[7]

Clarify the meaning. Do not use ambiguous words or phrases, be specific, and use simple words whenever possible to make the document as readable as possible. Use a readability formula to ensure that you are writing at the educational level of your audience.

Use variety. Alternate short sentences with longer ones to break the monotony. Use frequent exhibits such as charts and graphs to illustrate complicated points and to prevent the composition from becoming page after page of gray matter.

Be precise. Say exactly what you mean in language your reader can easily understand. Don't use jargon, clichés, trendy or casual language. Avoid the use of too many glowing superlatives that you may have to prove or apologize for later.

Review your logic. After you have checked the grammar, punctuation, spelling, and other editorial considerations, pause for a final review of your logic. Make sure your line of reasoning is easily followed, all the important elements are covered, and the length of each section is in accordance with its importance in the overall composition. Make sure your recommendations are realistic and reasonable. Don't confuse your reader with too many unimportant recommendations.

Call for action. Include a call for action so your reader understands exactly what you expect him to do after reading the document. Offer to provide additional information if it is necessary or of interest and let your reader know how to respond to your call for action. Should he telephone, write a letter, or initial and return the report to indicate agreement with the findings and recommendations? The action step is the payoff for all your efforts in research, writing, editing, and producing the document. Don't cheat yourself out of success with vague or uncertain action requests.

6

Sparkle, Snap, and Pizzazz: Making Your Writing Interesting

"In Hollywood, the woods are full of people that learned to write, but evidently can't read. If they could read their stuff, they'd stop writing."

Will Rogers

Advertising agencies continually study the effectiveness of their copywriting in an ongoing effort to outmaneuver the competition and get the reader's attention. It is a never-ending battle. The public is fickle, and its needs and interests constantly change. To get the reader's attention a writer must be sensitive to those changes.

This is especially difficult in a consumer-oriented society such as ours, where every reader is bombarded with hundreds of messages daily. To cope with that problem advertising writers developed a strategy they called *positioning*. During the early 1970s two admen, Jack Trout and Al Ries, wrote a series of articles for *Advertising Age* in which they defined positioning and demonstrated how it works.[1]

They pointed out this old advertising word now relates to what goes on in the prospective customer's mind, not in the marketplace. In short, we already have a list of products or ideas that we relate to other ideas or products that are new to us. We already have a belief about various products, and we rank them according to attributes they possess.

It is not easy to change our convictions or the position a product occupies in our mind. Cadillac found that out when it began marketing small cars. We consumers always related the Cadillac name with bigness and luxury. A small, economical Cadillac simply didn't compute, and it took years for small Cadillacs to become big sellers.

This advertising information can be used to great advantage in the production of business communications. The best way to get and hold a report reader's attention is to relate it to his situation and to things he already knows.

If you want to make what you have to say interesting to your reader, the best way to do so is to relate the topic of the report to its effect on him and his position in the company. Emphasize the benefits to him and the results of following your suggestions, not the clever methods you used to arrive at this conclusion.

Dr. Kenneth McFarland said in a speech to the National Sales Executives convention, "In psychology we say everyone has his aura of interest. That's a hard way of saying that everyone lives in a circle. If you want to do business with him you get in the circle with him. . . . Everyone has his aura of aspiration. The butcher boy, for example, doesn't want to be mayor—he'd just like to own the butcher shop some day. So, you don't talk to him about city hall, you help him own the butcher shop, and you're in the circle with him."[2]

So it is with communications of any sort. You have to get into the circle with your reader—to look at the situation from his point of view. And, as Dr. McFarland eloquently pointed out, your reader is the best expert in the world on his situation.

This approach to writing obviously relates more to persuasive communications than to those designed to inform; nevertheless, looking at any document from the reader's point of view can only help your effort. If your assignment is simply writing a report without making recommendations, your writing will appeal to your reader a great deal more if you present only information that is important to your reader, in a logical sequence.

There are techniques that the business writer can borrow from advertising and feature writers that will help make your writing interesting.

SOME TIPS FROM COMMERCIAL WRITERS

Relate It to Something Your Reader Already Knows

As advertising copywriters employ the concept of positioning to establish a product position in the minds of their customers, the same principle can be used in writing reports, memos, proposals, and letters. Give examples of how this technique or idea was used successfully in other areas of the company, or compare the savings to previous year's expenses, or relate it to the budget. All these techniques will help your reader place the information you are providing in perspective, and relating it to what he already knows will help him remember what you said.

Lead with the Most Important Information

Newspaper writers use a technique they call the *inverted pyramid* style of writing. This means simply your beginning, or lead, sentence should capsulize the entire message, or the most important fact should be presented first and the rest of the facts in descending order of importance. This strategy allows the reader to get the gist of the story by reading only the first few paragraphs. Of course, in the newspaper business there is an added benefit of ending the story with the least important information: layout artists can cut the story from the bottom up to make it fit the page without drastically altering the story.

Leading with your best material dictates that you spend the necessary time polishing the lead until it virtually leaps off the page at the reader. Whatever you say afterward will be enhanced by your first sentence.

Help Your Reader Visualize the Event

Don't just summarize the facts in a report; use some of the actual comments of those involved to let the reader visualize what happened. If, for example, you are reporting the results of a survey, use some of the more interesting responses to illustrate the respondents' feelings about the topic.

If you are reporting the results of a meeting, use actual quotes to spice up what might otherwise be drab minutes. If there was a spirited discussion about the approach to solving a problem, say so and let the speakers say it in their own words. *Example:*

Late in the meeting a spirited discussion ensued that focused on whether to cut costs by reducing the payroll or cutting travel expenses:

Jones: I am violently opposed to laying off employees to solve a short-term profit problem. After all, these are people's lives and careers we are talking about. We can all cut our travel budgets 25 percent and have the same savings.

Smith: Our first responsibility is to earn a profit for our shareholders, and to do so we must send our salesmen to call on customers. We cannot cut travel budgets. I am sympathetic to those we must let go, but we are not a social welfare agency. We are a profit-making company!

Of course, depending on the speakers and their positions in the company, you may wish to use some discretion in how you report the discussion. Your writing might be interesting enough to place you in the group to be terminated.

Focus on the Idea, Not the Language

As discussed earlier, simple, plain language will help you communicate with your reader, but it will also help make your writing more interesting. Words are the tools you use to convey your ideas and should not be so showy and pretentious that they become more visible than the ideas.

Lewis Mumford put it this way: "A book has one leg on immortality's trophy when the words are for children and the meanings are for men."[3] The words should fade into the background and allow the ideas to stand in the spotlight.

Read Other Reports, Proposals, Memos, and Letters

If you are like most people in business today, you probably receive mountains of paperwork every day that you scan if the topic interests you and toss if it doesn't. Take a critical look at those that are interesting and those that are not. Analyze the techniques that the writer used to help get and hold your attention; then use those ideas in your own writing.

Keep a file of well-written documents that you can use as a ready reference source. Examples of good proposals, for example, may save a lot of time when you are searching for effective ways to organize and present the material.

Make the Layout and Form Consistent with Your Plans

In every type of written communication, how the words look on the page will influence your reader's response. If you want to keep your readers interested, use the visual arrangement on the page to pull your reader into your message.

Advertising copywriters and television scriptwriters can rely heavily on elaborate graphics, special effects, and photographs to get the readers' attention. As a business writer your challenge is to stimulate interest with considerably fewer visual tools. Alternating short and long sentences; using charts and graphs, headlines, underscoring, bullets, numbers, and dashes; and indenting paragraphs are all effective ways to call attention to certain key portions of the document.

Prethink Your Message

In *The Feature Writer's Handbook*[4] author Stewart Harral advises aspiring writers to give an idea time to develop rather than rushing to the typewriter and starting to pound on the keys the moment an idea flutters by. He counsels writers to think out the angles, the outline, the specific devices, and to visualize the completed article.

If your message is firmly fixed in your mind, committing it to paper will be considerably easier. When you have to think as you go about what you want to write it is easy to derail your train of thought.

Use Plenty of Actual Examples or Situations

Case studies are frequently used in technical articles to help the reader better understand how the concept related to an actual situation and to help him relate the idea to his own situation. Very often, however, you must tell your reader specifically how the idea applies, particularly if the process involves several steps.

The use of examples or case studies can be especially effective in proposals to demonstrate how your service or product or idea will benefit the user. The method of presenting case studies might even follow a standard format for simplicity and ease of use.

Peat, Marwick, Mitchell & Co., the international accounting firm, always includes a case study of a successful business development effort in its *Practice Development Report,* an internal newsletter that focuses on the firm's business development activities. (See example on page 65.)

If It's Worth Doing . . .

Finally, if you are going to write anything, give it your best effort. If you are writing a memo about something you consider trivial, or if you hate to write anything, the chances are good that that message will come through to your reader loud and clear.

Even if you are not personally interested in the subject, if you have followed the rules of good composition and written the best document you could, your reader will recognize the quality of the presentation.

Practice Development Report

Peat
Marwick
Mitchell
& Co.

For the Management Group

September 14, 1981
Vol. 1 No. 3

Insight

The Japanese Practice is unique, yet it illustrates many of the problems and opportunities in marketing. It is highly segmented but crosses many business lines. Product packaging and delivery also must conform to differing cultural patterns. *Practice Development Report (PDR)* talked with Yukuo Takenaka, national director of the Japanese Practice in the United States, who will become the director of "Project Japan" effective October 1 and will spearhead Peat Marwick International's effort to develop Japanese clients on a worldwide basis.

What's New

Insight: Yukuo Takenaka Talks About Japanese Business
Page 1

Publications Briefs
Page 2

Marketing Tools
Page 2

At a Glance
Page 2

Government Watch
Page 3

Case Study: International Harvester
Page 3

Bits and Pieces
Page 4

Marketing Focus
Page 6

Calendar
Page 6

"Project Japan" is Peat Marwick International's marketing effort to carve out a large chunk of business from Japanese firms on a worldwide basis. Project Japan was started two years ago and has enjoyed a modest success. However, Japanese Practice coordinators around the world felt the Firm could do better. "Its initial objectives were sound," says Yukuo Takenaka, "but results did not fully meet our expectations."

Peat Marwick set up shop in Japan in 1946 to handle multinational companies doing business there. The business environment and the status of the accounting profession in Japan inhibited our efforts to establish close relationships with Japanese companies. Things began to change, however, as Japanese firms became multinational companies in their own right and required international accounting and audit procedures to obtain financing or to meet local reporting requirements.

"Because of this, our business with Japanese firms developed much more rapidly in the United States than in Japan," Takenaka says, noting that some 600 companies are served by the Firm. And he looks to these Japanese subsidiaries here as prime resources to help Peat Marwick interface with parent company executives in Japan.

Each country has submitted a list of target companies. "I will work the Tokyo connection and make certain there is a Japanese-speaking professional servicing the companies in each country," he says.

"I plan to spend half of my time in Japan and the remainder in Los Angeles to discharge my responsibilities for the U.S. firm. Project Japan will have its own offices set up next door to our affiliate in Japan, Showa Audit Corporation. We will meet frequently with the top Japanese businessmen to establish closer relationships and to wave the Peat Marwick banner. This way we hope to identify the companies most likely to seek international investment and financing and to make our case for serving all their subsidiaries."

Takenaka, an ebullient Japanese who became a U.S. citizen, begins his job with one success already. His long-term connection with the U.S. operations of Nippon Miniature Bearing (NMB) Co., Ltd. (an aggressive, growing conglomerate), has already borne fruit. "They are giving me a present for my new responsibility," he says. "NMB has agreed to use Peat Marwick for all its international operations (United States, United Kingdom, France, West Germany, Hong Kong, Taiwan, Singapore, and Thailand) and to engage the Firm in Japan when it seeks international financing. Our worldwide fees for NMB will be quite substantial."

Takenaka believes that Japanese companies are finding it more convenient to deal with one worldwide accounting firm and that they naturally will engage a firm that has a good understanding of Japanese business and strong language capabilities. Peat Marwick is clearly one of the leaders in this area, he asserts, but he adds that we need to strengthen our competitive position continually. "We have to see to it that our services to Japanese clients in each country are coordinated by professionals who speak the language and understand Japanese business practices. Project Japan clearly differentiates us from the competition because of the enthusiasm shown by PMI firms for working together to pursue this exciting opportunity," Takenaka says.

THE USE OF ANECDOTES OR HUMOR

If there is any good general advice about using humor in business writing, it would be: don't. In most cases, humor isn't appropriate and will serve only to make the rest of your message appear frivolous.

In some instances humor may provide needed relief or divert your reader's attention from the negative aspects of your message. Be very careful, however, that what you say does not backfire by offending your reader. Never use ethnic, sexist, or off-color humor. Telling such stories is bad enough in a business environment, but putting them in writing is unforgivable.

Here is an example of how you might use light humor to soften the blow of bad news:[5]

MEMORANDUM

To: S. A. Cypert   Date: August 1, 19xx

From: R. D. Nicholas   Enclosures: (None)

Subject: Utilities Expense

Did you hear the one about the old farmer who was once asked by a young lad how he became so rich?

"It's a long story," said the old man, "and while I'm telling it I may as well save the candle." And he put it out.

"You need not tell the story," said the youth. "I understand."

If the utilities expenses in your plant continue the way they are going, we may have to send the old farmer up to tell you how to get rich.

Seriously, Sam, you may want to investigate this cost. In the past three months your electric bills have increased more than 30 percent, which is very unusual for the summertime.

Please let me know what you find to be the cause of the increase.

If the recipient has just completed an exhaustive study to try to determine the cause of the problem, which he initiated long before he received your memo, he probably will not get a very big laugh from it. If, on the other hand, the problem had gone unnoticed, he may appreciate your gently bringing it to his attention.

Therein lies the risk. You don't know how your reader will receive your attempt at wit or humor. Tastes vary, and one person's hilarity is another's sarcasm. Humorist Art Buchwald once said the trouble with writing satire is that either people don't understand what you are saying or they believe you. In business writing you neither want your reader to misunderstand you nor to think you flippant. Use humor sparingly.

If you do use humor, it is better to make yourself, rather than the reader, the butt of the joke. Otherwise you may come across as poking fun at your reader, which is sure to alienate him.

One of the better examples of the use of humor comes from the best advertising specialties salesman I have ever known. Elliott Rubin sends a monthly mailer to 130 or so selected customers and always has a sales pitch for the novelty item enclosed in the mailing—and tells a couple of jokes.

Elliott gets the reader on his side right away by poking fun at himself for telling this groaner in the first place. If he uses ethnic humor, it is usually about people of his own heritage and never biting sarcasm. The jokes are gentle jabs, not body blows. See the example on page 68.

The most important element in the success of this mailing piece is that everyone who receives it knows Elliot well. They are his good customers, and he sees them several times a year. He knows how every person on his list will react to his jokes.

It may be that the subject of your letter or memo lends itself naturally to the use of humor. Very few of us are blessed with such happy conditions, but John T. Flaherty is an exception. As chief of the division of sewer design for New York City, one of his responsibilities is to answer queries about alligators in the Big Apple's sewers.

Two of Mr. Flaherty's letters are reproduced here with permission. I am respecting his request that it might be a good idea to withhold the identity of the individual inquirers, considering, as he said, "the nature of some of the inquiries."

The first is his response to a New Yorker who wrote saying that he disagreed with a coworker who insists an alligator that has

Here's an advertising specialty that will be used with real consistency. People in the business world are always traveling. Why not keep your message in front of them. It can't hurt! By God...We go to trade shows, sales meetings...our sales people travel. Heck, this is a great idea that will get your advertising message across.

Do you realize that there is a law that says you must have a luggage tag on your luggage when you travel? Hell...I tie one on the inside and one on the outside handle...just in case. Have you ever lost your luggage? What an empty feeling!

This luggage tag is also a great traffic builder at tradeshows, a great sales hand out, a tremendous in-house promotion for company employees that are taking vacations, and a terrific idea as a direct mail piece to induce your customer, client, prospect or suspect, to open the envelope, because of the bulk. Heck...you did!

You know...If you've never used a specialty advertising product in a direct mail program, then you've missed the boat. Call me, and we'll talk about it. I'll even ask you to visit our newly expanded "Idea Showroom", and I'll show you some truly "Great Ideas".

I've convinced you and now you want the price breakdown on this great luggage tag. Here goes....

250	500	1000	2500	5000	10,000 pcs.
.69	.66	.59	.57	.52	.46 ea.

Ridiculous...Huh? Luggage tags are available in blue, white, green, yellow, black, red. Cello bagged individually.

You say that you're not ready for the "JOKE OF THE MONTH" and that you can't handle it so early in the morning? Sorry...Here tis...

> The rabbi and the priest were having a friendly discussion. "Tell me the truth, rabbi," the priest nudged him, "have you ever committed a sin against your faith?" The rabbi thought it over. "Well," he admitted, "once a long time ago, before I became a rabbi, I ate a piece of pork."
> The two sat in silence. Then, "Have you ever sinned, Father?" asked the rabbi.
> The priest grinned. "Before becoming a priest, I had an affair with a woman."
> More silence. Then, "Sure beats pork," said the rabbi.

Oh, well...call me and we'll talk "Ideas". Have I got some Great Ideas for you!

Advertisingly yours,

ELLIOTT RUBIN
1633 Ravine Lane
Highland Park, Illinois 60035
(312) 432-9060

lived in a sewer for a long period of time does not change color. His friend, the writer says, believes the pigmentation of the alligator would become much lighter and turn almost white in some cases. He goes on to say that his daughter's college professor agrees with his coworker that the color would change, and the writer would like Mr. Flaherty to resolve the disagreement. The following letter is his reply.

Dear Mr._____:

I have read with fascination your letter
concerning the great debate that is raging among
yourself, your co-worker, and your daughter's
college professor concerning the effects that long
habitation in the city's sewer system would have
on the pigmentation of an alligator. What is fas-
cinating is that the three of you (as well as your
daughter, for all I know) appear to take it for
granted that there is a resident population of
alligators in our sewers.

I hate to have to be the one to play the
role of wet blanket, but I am afraid that your
premise is faulty. There are no alligators
resident in the New York City sewer system. I
could cite you many cogent, logical reasons why
the sewer system is not a fit habitat for an
alligator, but suffice it to say that, in the
twenty-eight years I have been in the sewer game,
neither I nor any of the thousands of men who have
worked to build, maintain, or repair the sewer
system have ever seen one, and a ten-foot, 800-
pound alligator in a sewer would be hard to miss.

Of course, following the thought that you

advance in your letter to its ultimate conclusion,
perhaps the pigmentation effect has been so radical
that they have been rendered invisible. Somehow,
though, I rather doubt it.

Very truly yours,

John T. Flaherty, P.E.
Chief, Division of Sewer Design
Bureau of Sewers

The second letter answers an Australian who remembers a
friend "who happened to mention the alligators in New York
sewers but had forgotten the source of his information." The
inquirer was skeptical at first, but having heard the story so often
was "now inclined to believe the reports." The Australian wrote
to Mayor Koch, who forwarded the missive to Mr. Flaherty with
a request to clarify the matter for the ambivalent Australian. This
is his response:

Dear Mr. _____:

Your letter of September 2, 19xx, to Mayor
Koch has been referred to me for reply as over the
years I appear to have become the repository of all
wisdom on this particular subject.

Your parenthetical mention of the "bunyips"
provides the perfect lead-in to the subject of my
letter, as both the bunyip and the New York City
sewer alligator have several points in common:

1. Both could be considered monsters in the
sense that they would probably arouse feelings of

desire only among their own kind. This is undoubt-
edly the case with the alligator.

2. Their habitats (swamps and lagoons) are
certainly alike.

3. There is, unfortunately, a third point of
similarity that renders the first two academic and
that is that they are both legendary.

The origins of the bunyip legend are unknown
to me. However, I can speculate as to the genesis
of the alligator myth. It is true that, in the
1950s, people brought home baby alligators from
such places as Florida (apparently, these people
did not view an alligator as a monster, at least
not until it grew beyond a certain size). How
widespread this practice was I have no way of
knowing, but I suspect it wasn't very.

How people disposed of these unwanted pets can
never be known for certain. Many probably took the
most obvious course and donated them to any of the
many zoological institutions in the New York City
area. Some may even have deposited a few into the
sewer system and then bragged about their feat to
their friends. Since stories of these types seldom
lose anything in the retelling, and since such a
story would be far too good to keep to oneself, a

few baby alligators who, for any number of reasons, probably did not survive have become a horde upon the city, and now, it appears, the tale has spread even to the Land Down Under.

One last point. Among the group of people who do not abet the spread of the alligator myth are the city's sewer workers. The reason for this is quite simple. They have never seen any.

Very truly yours,

John T. Flaherty, P.E.
Chief, Division of Sewer Design
Bureau of Sewers

THE CLOSE

In sales every scrap of information, every inflection of the salesperson's voice is leading up to the big moment of truth—the close. It is the moment when the prospective client or customer says yes or no to the sales presentation.

Every business communication should be equally directed toward a "close" or final disposition of the matter at hand.

If your intent is to get action from your reader, tell him how you would like him to respond and provide a response vehicle. If you are providing information for the purpose of analysis and no action is necessary, tell your reader so. After he has finished reading your document he should never have to ask: What's next?

Direct mail experts offer formulas for ensuring success of mass mailings that are equally successful in written communications. Richard H. Stansfield's epic tome, the *Advertising Manager's Handbook*,[6] selects two from the scores that have become available as direct mailing evolved into a respectable advertising medium.

Victor Schwab's AAPPA formula:

A—Get *attention.*
A—Show people an *advantage.*

P—*Prove* it.

P—*Persuade* people to grasp this advantage.

A—Ask for *action*.

The other is attributed to Bob Stone, a direct mail and marketing expert and *Advertising Age* columnist. Stone offers this formula:

1. Promise a benefit in your headline or first paragraph—*your most important benefit.*
2. Immediately enlarge on your most important benefit.
3. Tell the reader *specifically* what he is going to get.
4. Back up your statement with *proof* and *endorsements.*
5. Tell the reader what he might lose if he doesn't act.
6. Rephrase your prominent benefits in your closing offer.
7. Incite action—*now.*

Either formula can readily be adapted to every form of business communications. Note the emphasis on benefits to the reader in the opening and closing sections. Reminding the reader about the benefits he will receive by adopting your idea or recommendation reinforces his reasons for buying what you are selling. There is never a better time to call for action than after summarizing and restating the benefits.

If possible, give your reader an easy response mechanism. In an officewide memo, for example, you may want to include a "fill in the blanks" return form at the bottom of the page for the reader to detach and return to you. *Example*:

```
To:   Joe Doakes

From: _____


 ⟨⟩  Count me in, Joe.  I want to help with the

     American Cancer Society Bike-a-thon.  I am

     interested in the following:

          ____ riding in the event

          ____ sponsoring a rider

          ____ working as a volunteer judge
```

It is always a good idea to eliminate the need for a response whenever it is practical and to make it easy for the reader to act on your request. *Example:*

● If I don't hear from you by March 1, I will assume you agree with my proposal and we will begin implementation immediately. [Caution: Be sure you allow enough time, and make sure you have an agreement beforehand with your reader. Don't let him find out when he returns from three weeks in Europe that you spent a million dollars on a project he knew nothing about because he didn't respond by March 1.]

● Please indicate your approval by initialing this memo and returning it to me.

● I would appreciate your telephoning me with your reaction to my report within two weeks.

● Let me know if you are planning to attend the meeting and I will ask my secretary to make reservations so we can travel together.

● Unless you advise me otherwise, I will expect you here at 10:00 on Thursday.

Summary

Whatever you do, don't let your message run out of space and end. "Close the sale" with a call for action that unmistakably identifies your intentions and persuades your reader to follow your recommendations. If your communication is designed to advise or inform, tell your reader that. Don't exchange any more correspondence than is necessary. Always make it easy for your reader to respond when a response is needed.

7

Visual Techniques to Grab the Reader

"The phenomenon I refer to . . . is the tidal wave of craving for convenience that is sweeping America. Today, convenience is the success factor of just about every type of produce and service that is showing steady growth."

Charles G. Mortimer

In business communication today advances in technology are being made so rapidly that it is difficult for the most practiced observer to fully understand the capability we have. Extensive data bases can be accessed by computer terminals that are not much larger than a conventional typewriter. Literally at your fingertips is complete information companies furnish to their shareholders and everything that has been published about a particular topic. (See Chapter 3 for more information about data bases available for research needs.)

There is no doubt that considerably more information is available today—about almost any topic we can imagine—than we can assimilate. Technology has enabled us to dish out far more than we can take in. As a result it is more important than ever to distill the message whenever possible and to arrange it in a fashion that can easily be scanned by the reader to determine which of the materials is most pertinent.

Newspapers accomplish the attention-getting aspect by varying the size of headlines, with the main story headlined across the front page and stories of lesser importance relegated to inside pages and given smaller headlines. The idea is to grab the reader's attention as he walks past the newsstand so he will purchase a newspaper.

FORMAT FEATURES

Business writers seldom use screaming headlines and large typefaces to get their readers' attention, but there are techniques that can be used to facilitate reading ease and enable your reader to scan your writing.

Spacing

How the report should look is not left to the discretion of the typist: it is the author's responsibility to instruct the typist or word processing operator how the finished report is to look. Some organizations have alleviated the problem and limited the decision-making process by publishing corporate manuals that describe precisely how the report is to be constructed. In fields in which specialists and experts issue frequent reports, technical manuals may include instructions for report format.

If you are bound by none of these constraints, you should let the report's end use determine its final appearance. If you are writing a report that will be distributed with a request for comment, you may wish to double-space it to allow room for reviewer's notes. Manuscripts are always double-spaced to allow space for editors and proofreaders to pencil instructions to the typesetters. If the report is the finished document that is to be distributed to a wide audience, you may wish to single-space it to limit its length and to give it the appearance of being "finished."

As author of the report, the option is yours. Some experts will insist that there are hard and fast rules that certain documents should be double-spaced while others must be single-spaced, but for every expert who advises you one way, there is a countering opinion from another expert who disagrees. Regardless of all the advice, you are the world's greatest expert on your particular situation. You know the customs in your company and how your readers are likely to react. Use the visual techniques that will help your reader get your message.

Indentation

If you double-space the document, you should indent paragraphs to let the reader know where the next paragraph begins. If you single-space, you should double-space between paragraphs and triple-space between headings and the beginning of the following paragraph. Many editors suggest indenting paragraphs in every situation to break up the text and to avoid the appearance of a page of continuous text, which is monotonous.

Margins

To get off to a good visual start, always leave plenty of space for margins in whatever you write. A general rule of thumb is to leave a one-inch margin at the top and sides of the page and about 1½ inches at the bottom for double-spaced copy. If you single-space, use a 1¼-inch margin for the sides and top and about 1½ inches at the bottom of the page. If you begin with a substantial margin, the rest of the techniques you use to make the report pleasing to the eye will be much more effective.

Before you instruct your typist or word processor operator about the margins you should work up an estimate of the document's total number of pages and decide how it will be bound. Lengthy reports and proposals may require extra space on the left side of the page for binding.

Headings

You may elect to use any combination of uppercase and lowercase headings, and they may be underlined or otherwise emphasized to draw attention to them. Ordinarily, main headings would use the most dominant form, and topics of lesser importance would be more subdued. Whatever combination you select, be consistent throughout.

Here are some examples of headings, in order of emphasis:

<u>UPPERCASE UNDERLINED</u>

UPPERCASE

<u>Uppercase and Lowercase Underlined</u>

Uppercase and Lowercase

Side Heads

Sometimes called *marginal headings*, side headings are usually uppercase and lowercase underlined. They should never be more dominant in subject matter or appearance than center or main headings.

Boxed Heads

So designated because of the visual "box" formed by surrounding text, boxed heads are an effective alternative. If you use word processing equipment, however, you should check with the operator to be sure your equipment can handle boxed heads and underlines efficiently.

Continuous Side Heads

You may wish to use continuous or *run-in* headings to emphasize minor points in the text. Be sure to allow about five spaces after the last word in the heading to distinguish it from the rest of the paragraph and always underline continuous side heads.

On page 79 is an example of the effective use of a variety of headings in a public relations activity report.

As this example demonstrates, lists of information can be made visually pleasing through the use of bullets. Instead of bullets, you may elect to use numbers, dashes, letters, or asterisks. In longer documents you may decide to use a combination to break the visual monotony.

With the sophisticated word processing equipment available, and easy-to-change fonts on conventional office typewriters, you may select different typefaces for emphasizing headings. If you are not familiar with type styles and which faces are commonly used together, stick to one typeface such as IBM Prestige Elite and the italics of the same typeface.

You may wish to highlight headings or key passages of the report with color. Several firms offer felt-tip highlighters in a variety of colors for this purpose. If you highlight, do so after the copies have been made. Most photocopiers print only black and white, and your color highlight may obliterate the key passages when the page is photocopied.

SELZ, SEABOLT & ASSOCIATES, INC.

International
Public Relations Counsel

221 North La Salle Street
Chicago, Illinois 60601
Phone: (312) 372-7090

To: Paul Fullmer

From: George Eisenhuth
             Mike Bruening

Subject: Client Activity Report

FEBRUARY ACTIVITIES REVIEW

The following is a report of our activities in behalf of our client, John Miller Manufacturing Co., Inc. As the client requested, we have concentrated our efforts on the firm's line of cooking grills.

Special Projects

- Submitted revised Dealer Demonstration Program for review and approval; put into production for distribution to dealers and distributors by Miller Manufacturing in early March.

- Reviewed cooperative program with Beef Council for Father's Day color page and provided the client with a cost estimate.

- Provided press kits for use by the client at the Canadian Hardware Show.

Media Contacts

- Distributed publicity releases on Miller Grills to American Building Supplies, Family Handyman, Canadian DIY, Home Goods Retailing, Home-owners How-To, Dealerscope, and Centre magazines.

- Contacted trade and consumer magazines to develop and encourage stories and interviews. Need to coordinate with client travel schedule.

Reports, Planning

- Reviewed public relations schedule for remainder of the year with client; final approval expected next week.
- Provided client with monthly activities report and clipping summary for February.

P Founding member of THE PINNACLE GROUP, INC.
Atlanta, Chicago, Houston, Los Angeles, Minneapolis, New York, San Francisco, Washington, Canada, Europe

CHARTS, GRAPHS, AND TABLES

We've heard the old saw "A picture is worth a thousand words" hundreds of times, yet when it comes to writing, we seem to lose sight of the advantages a good illustration can give us in helping readers understand what we are trying to convey.

The more complex the subject matter, the more imperative it is to help the reader conceptualize the topic through the use of charts, graphs, and tables that show at a glance comparisons of pertinent data that would otherwise be almost impossible to plow through and organize mentally.

Some frequent users of charts in technical fields have designed charts that are unique to their field as a shorthand to understanding the various processes. Computer programmers, for example, use flowcharts to illustrate the flow of information.

Line Graphs

A simple form of graph is the line graph, which is generally used to display changes over a period of time, with time plotted on the horizontal axis and units of measurement or values plotted on the vertical axis. (See graph below.)

To show comparative information or data in the same line graph, use different graphic representations such as dotted lines, dashes, or solid lines to designate different elements.

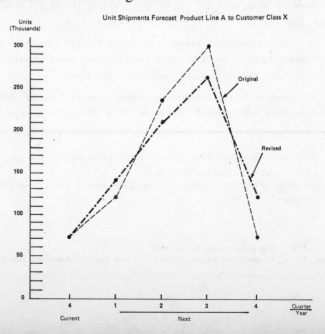

A line graph can be used to illustrate several components in the same chart. Because of the construction, however, it is possible to illustrate only one type of information. The elements can simply be stacked one on the other, or the design can be quite elaborate. (See illustration below.) The different patterns used to illustrate various elements of the graph can be purchased with a pressure-sensitive adhesive backing from art supply stores or ordered by mail from various distributors. This easy-to-use material can be cut to the desired size and shape and then adhered to the page in place.

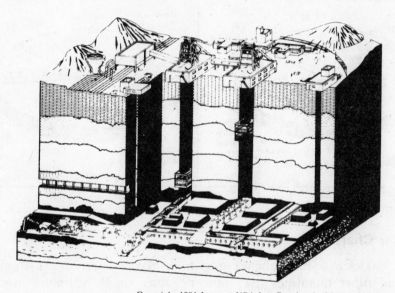

Copyright 1981 Letraset USA Inc. Reprinted with permission.

Pie Charts

Pie charts are especially effective in displaying the division of parts of the whole. "Slices" of the pie are sized according to their relationship to the whole pie and other slices.

Conversions from numbers to degrees of a circle can be difficult if you have trouble remembering mathematical formulas. To convert percentages to degrees, multiply the percent expressed in decimals by 360, the number of degrees in a circle. *Example:*

To determine the size of the slice that represents 7 percent of the total, multiply $360 \times .07 = 25.2$ degrees. Use a protractor to plot the solution on your pie chart, beginning at the 12:00 position so the eye will follow the graph around as it would the face of a clock. (See pie chart below.)

If you are unsure of your calculations, use the conversion chart on page 83.

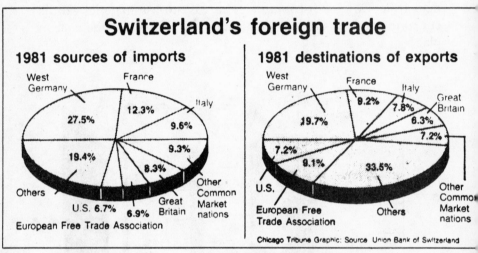

Chicago Tribune Graphic Copyrighted 1982. Used with permission

Bar Charts

Bar charts are frequently used to display financial information and other quantities over time or other simple variables over fixed units of measurement such as distances or dollars.

Corporations use bar charts to illustrate sales and earnings comparisons in annual reports to shareholders and often incorporate bar charts in the overall design of the report, such as the McDonough Co. 1979 Annual Report cover shown on page 84.

Bar charts may be subdivided to illustrate the elements of the whole, such as in the UAL, Inc. Sources of Airline 1980 Operating Revenues Dollar chart on page 85.

CONVERSION CHART

Percent	Degrees	Percent	Degrees	Percent	Degrees	Percent	Degrees
1	3.6	26	93.6	51	183.6	76	273.6
2	7.2	27	97.2	52	187.2	77	277.2
3	10.8	28	100.8	53	190.8	78	280.8
4	14.4	29	104.4	54	194.4	79	284.4
5	18.0	30	108.0	55	198.0	80	288.0
6	21.6	31	111.6	56	201.6	81	291.6
7	25.2	32	115.2	57	205.2	82	295.2
8	28.8	33	118.8	58	208.8	83	298.8
9	32.4	34	122.4	59	212.4	84	302.4
10	36.0	35	126.0	60	216.0	85	306.0
11	39.6	36	129.6	61	219.6	86	309.6
12	43.2	37	133.2	62	223.2	87	313.2
13	46.8	38	136.8	63	226.8	88	316.8
14	50.4	39	140.4	64	230.4	89	320.4
15	54.0	40	144.0	65	234.0	90	324.0
16	47.6	41	147.6	66	237.6	91	327.6
17	61.2	42	151.2	67	241.2	92	331.2
18	64.8	43	154.8	68	244.8	93	334.8
19	68.4	44	158.4	69	248.4	94	338.4
20	72.0	45	162.0	70	252.0	95	342.0
21	75.6	46	165.6	71	255.6	96	345.6
22	79.2	47	169.2	72	259.2	97	349.2
23	82.8	48	172.8	73	262.8	98	352.8
24	86.4	49	176.4	74	266.4	99	356.4
25	90.0	50	180.0	75	270.0	100	360.0

McDONOUGH CO.
Annual Report January 31, 1979

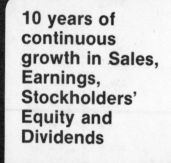

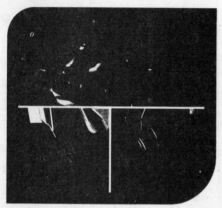

Sales
(Dollars in millions)

10 years of continuous growth in Sales, Earnings, Stockholders' Equity and Dividends

Earnings Per Share
(Dollars)

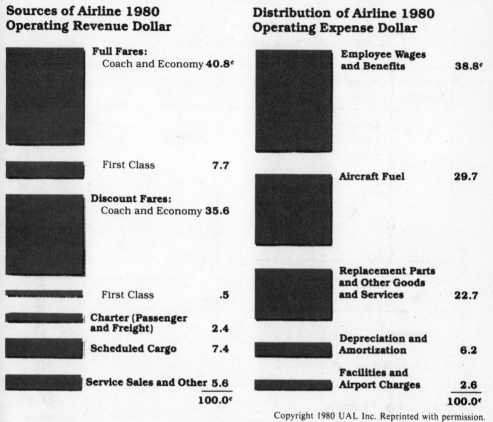

Sources of Airline 1980 Operating Revenue Dollar

Full Fares:
Coach and Economy **40.8¢**

First Class **7.7**

Discount Fares:
Coach and Economy **35.6**

First Class **.5**

Charter (Passenger and Freight) **2.4**

Scheduled Cargo **7.4**

Service Sales and Other **5.6**

100.0¢

Distribution of Airline 1980 Operating Expense Dollar

Employee Wages and Benefits **38.8¢**

Aircraft Fuel **29.7**

Replacement Parts and Other Goods and Services **22.7**

Depreciation and Amortization **6.2**

Facilities and Airport Charges **2.6**

100.0¢

Tables

When the data to be presented are long and complex, you may want to include as part of the text a complete table for the reader to use as a specific reference, or you may wish to include tables in appendices as supporting documentation for your narrative. In either case the construction of tables is essentially the same; however, references should give the reader specific information you are trying to convey if you use it in the text or refer the reader to the appendix for more information.

Tables usually have an identifying title, a left-side heading to identify the frame of reference, a subheading, and individual column headings. The total is usually presented in the right-hand column or at the bottom of each of the individual columns, as appropriate. All tables should include a source. (If *you* gathered the data, the source would be identified as *primary*). Space should also be provided for footnotes.

Example:

Table Number and Title				
Side Heading	Subheading			
	Column Heading	Column Heading	Column Heading	Column Heading
Total				
Footnotes:				
Source notation:				

Alternative Example:

Table Number and Title				
Side Heading	Subheading			
	Column Heading	Column Heading	Column Heading	Total
Comparison (average, normal, etc.)				
Footnotes:				
Source notation:.				

Table Preparation Tips

- Remember that the purpose of the table is to illustrate. Make it informative and easy to identify the key elements.
- Use averages, subtotals, and totals wherever they help the reader understand better.
- Use symbols to identify footnoted information to avoid confusion or possible misunderstandings as to whether footnote numbers are part of the table.
- Make sure units of measurement are identified clearly.
- Use dashes or "not available" (na) where data is not available instead of zeros, which imply a different meaning.

The table below is a good example.

HEATING DEGREE-DAY DATA FOR CHICAGO

Season	Sept.	Oct.	Nov.	Dec.	Jan.	Feb.	Mar.	Apr.	May	June	July	Aug.	Tot.
1948-49	49	419	656	1074	1134	1039	854	515	184	16	0	2	5942
1949-50	160	276	745	1032	1095	1078	987	699	174	41	3	15	6305
1950-51	65	225	913	1283	1052	915	547	165	44	0	0	4	6616
1951-52	114	342	957	1196	1163	942	917	419	223	10	0	6	6289
1952-53	85	502	660	1005	1098	924	789	544	187	15	0	0	5809
1953-54	62	208	612	1022	1149	761	922	354	275	34	0	0	5399
1954-55	31	329	666	1020	1238	1007	854	239	112	47	0	0	5543
1955-56	43	300	864	1205	1123	1025	878	532	212	35	3	3	6223
1956-57	86	153	724	993	1425	877	842	473	228	23	0	0	5824
1957-58	89	397	736	941	1192	1253	890	406	149	61	0	4	6118
1958-59	67	255	659	1315	1437	1083	853	466	114	12	0	0	6261
1959-60	62	406	939	898	1137	1132	1192	374	221	39	0	0	6400
1960-61	26	301	657	1225	1284	853	741	612	265	31	3	2	6000
1961-62	77	293	718	1204	1450	1091	935	480	117	28	1	1	6395
1962-63	112	276	674	1234	1600	1277	720	383	225	26	2	6	6535
1963-64	50	98	579	1454	1090	1017	894	419	83	23	0	0	5843
1964-65	101	423	633	1160	1250	1048	1069	515	105	32	0	0	6030
1965-66	99	350	683	879	1437	1031	761	511	314	33	0	0	6098
1966-67	83	363	653	1116	1113	1198	814	434	330	10	0	0	6114
1967-68	104	381	803	1027	1243	1108	666	360	218	14	0	0	5924
1968-69	41	331	691	1093	1336	966	941	406	197	101	0	0	6103
1969-70	56	390	777	1118	1475	1071	919	406	149	27	0	0	6388
1970-71	79	293	723	1032	1413	1023	903	482	257	10	0	0	6215
1971-72	72	146	683	871	1311	1139	929	539	177	78	0	0	5945
1972-73	93	454	818	1224	1118	967	609	489	284	0	0	1	5613
1973-74	70	232	685	1158	1230	1058	803	397	272	51	0	2	5958
1974-75	157	360	715	1041	1144	1058	947	638	142	22	2	2	6227
1975-76	155	279	532	1029	1389	840	674	405	264	16	0	0	5583
1976-77	88	520	960	1398	1695	1059	622	344	264	16	0	0	6955
1977-78	51	402	728	1242	1517	1346	1003	508	272	36	4	1	7110
1978-79	50	410	671	1199	1628	1345	910	606	216	28	2	13	7078
1979-80	61	367	726	951	1281	1254	995	558	198	83	0	3	6477
1980-81	71	511	746	1140	1308	1031	846	397	313	6	8	6	6383
1981-82	82	135	405	665	1162								
Normal	57	316	738	1132	1262	1053	874	453	208	70	0	0	6163
Av. pct. fuel consumption 65-yr. basis	.5	5.4	12	18	20	17	14	8	4	1			

Source: Building Managers Assn. of Chicago. Although the official Chicago reporting station was moved to O'Hare Field on 1-1-80, for purposes of continuity this report will continue to reflect Midway data.

Maps

Maps are frequently used in reports and proposals to illustrate related locations such as plants and sales offices or to represent geographic distribution of resources or statistical data. UAL, Inc., for example, in its annual report uses a map to show United Airlines' new routes:

——— New Routes 1980

- - - - New Routes 1981

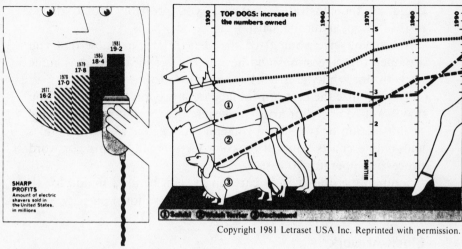

Custom Commercial Artwork

On occasion you may find it necessary to include an illustration to explain a difficult concept or simply to draw the reader's attention to a significant point. Your firm's art department may be able to help you, or you may elect to engage a free-lance artist to devise an illustration or two for you. In either event, if you are not familiar with costs involved, ask for an estimate.

Graphic artists, like other service suppliers, have only their time to sell and usually provide estimates based on the amount of time they expect to spend developing the idea for the illustration and putting it into final, finished, reproduction-quality form.

If you don't have any idea how to express the information visually, tell the artist your problem and ask for two or three alternatives from which you can select one that suits your needs best. Then leave the artist alone and let him apply his talent and experience to your problem. Don't peer over his shoulder and offer suggestions for improvement. Most of us don't do our best thinking with someone looking over our shoulder and second-guessing us, and if you waste your artist's time, you cost yourself money.

If you do have a firm idea in mind, make a sketch of your idea for presenting the material and give it to your artist along with the data necessary to complete the illustration or chart. Don't be embarrassed about the quality of your sketch. Artists are used to dealing with clients who are unskilled at graphics. After all, if you could do the illustration yourself, you probably would do so instead of engaging the artist.

When you give your artist the sketch, let him know that you are open for suggestions and new and better ideas. He may come up with one while he is working on your idea.

To minimize the cost of producing your report or proposal, you may want to ask your artist to design a cover and a key drawing or illustration or two. Then you can produce the rest of the tables and simple charts yourself or ask your secretary, typist, or word processing operator to assist.

Simple line drawings or cartoon art can be used to add life to an otherwise plain chart, as in the examples shown on page 89.

Stock Artwork

If you are a frequent producer of reports and proposals, you may want to keep a stock of art supplies and materials that you can use to improve the visual appearance of your work. After you have invested the time to produce information that is relevant and correct, applied your judgment and knowledge to solving the problems, and written it in a fashion to make it interesting to the reader, a small investment in graphics will pay big dividends in readership.

Several firms specialize in the production of art supplies that are relatively easy to use and require a minimum of time and effort to produce. "Clip art" is available with a variety of subject matter and of suitable quality for reproduction. Illustrations can be clipped and pasted in place for printing or photocopying. Rub-off or transfer lettering comes in a wide range of type sizes and styles and may be transferred to a blank sheet by rubbing the surface with an ordinary pen or pencil.

Rub-off lettering manufacturers also provide symbols that can be transferred in the same manner for use in pictograms that use symbols instead of lines or bars, or "pert charts."

8

Proposals—The Planning Process

"The most important secret of salesmanship is finding out what the other fellow wants, then helping him find the best way to get it."

Frank Bettger

You may very well ask yourself, "What's the point of spending a lot of time and money to develop a proposal to someone else in my company? We both share the same goals, and we should work together for the success of our firm."

I doubt that anyone would argue with that philosophy. Certainly, I wouldn't. But in business, philosophy and practice are seldom constant companions.

Within any organization that has agreed-upon profit, growth and expansion, management development, or other goals, there are as many ideas about how to reach those goals as there are individuals involved. And the higher they rank in the organization, the more responsibility they bear for achieving those goals and the more likely they are to trust their own instincts.

What this means is they will do what is necessary to get the job done. If people within the organization can help them reach that end, they will use company personnel. If they cannot find the support internally, they will get it from outside suppliers. And for every service or support department in any company there is an

91

outside supplier who will promise to do the job faster and cheaper than the inside support group can do it.

Most employees of the same firm would prefer to use company people to do the job whenever possible. They are, accordingly, predisposed to buying from you, so your selling job should be easier than that of your competitor, but they still must be sold.

In any selling process at least four sales are actually made: the salesman, the company, the product or service, and the service or support of that product or service are all sold. In internal selling you have already made some of these "sales within the sale." The prospective "client" should already be sold on the company and, to varying degrees, on the other three as well.

I singled out service departments because they are miniature companies within companies that sell a service to an internal clientele. Others in line functions must also sell their ideas to budget committees, to owners of the business, or to others who must decide how to spend a finite amount of funds on an almost infinite number of projects.

Here is where the proposal comes in. Your proposal is your messenger, your salesman in meetings at which funding is won or lost or projects are approved or rejected.

In such situations those charged with decision making have to develop some system for screening proposed projects. What usually happens is that they look for reasons to throw out a proposal to reduce the number of proposals under consideration to a manageable figure. How the idea is presented and how well the proposal persuades are very important criteria for retaining instead of throwing out projects. It is safe to say that a proposal may not get the assignment or the funding for you, but it can certainly lose it for you.

If you are a service department, any number of outside suppliers are constantly calling on your clientele, trying to dislodge you so they can sell services like yours. This is another compelling reason to produce the best possible proposal.

In this situation *best* doesn't necessarily mean *longest*. There was a time when a proposal's length seemed to be in direct proportion to the fees or budget requested, but with the information explosion that has come upon business in recent years some readers have started to believe that less is better. As author of the proposal you play an important role in determining whether to issue a two-page memo describing the service you are selling or the project you are proposing or a full-scale proposal with all the bells and whistles on it.

When big projects or large amounts of money are at stake, seldom does one person bear full responsibility for developing and issuing a proposal. In firms where proposals to clients and prospects are the lifeblood of the business (such as consulting and engineering firms) teams of specialists are assembled, proposal staffing assignments are made, a proposal manager is appointed, budgets are established, and a proposal strategy is developed before a single word is ever put on paper. If you are doing the job solo, it simply means you have several roles in the proposal's development.

THE SECRET OF SUCCESSFUL PROPOSALS

In almost every venture that ends successfully, seeds for success are sown in the beginning—the planning—stage. With winning proposals this is especially true. The plan you develop, and the theme of the proposal that evolves from your plan, is the foundation on which the success or failure of your proposal rests.

The time you spend in planning your approach to the project and analyzing your audience's needs and interests is the most important time you will spend on the entire project. Don't skimp on it.

As soon as you have determined that you are going to issue a proposal for this project, your first action should be to call a meeting of everyone involved in the proposal effort. The purpose of the meeting is to map out a definite strategy to meet the proposal's goal, to make assignments, and to establish deadlines.

Strategy

By far the most important aspect of the meeting is the strategy session. This should be an open discussion about various avenues that could be taken to achieve the goal. If the intent of the proposal is to sell corporate support services to an operating division, for example, the strategy should focus on both real and perceived needs of that division's management. Other alternatives open to the division 'should be explored, and advantages in dealing with corporate should be emphasized. Strengths of the group providing the services should be identified and listed for future reference. Finally, from this meeting should emerge a theme or proposal approach that those responsible for producing it can follow throughout its development.

Staff Assignments

Producing a winning proposal, particularly a large one, involves a great deal of effort and coordination. The first assignment to be made is to put one person in charge of the entire proposal effort. That person is responsible for coordinating the efforts of all others involved in the project and making sure it is issued on time. Various other duties are assigned to appropriate people. Portions of the proposal may need to be written by technical experts, it may require review by legal counsel, project staffing considerations must be addressed, and someone should be assigned to edit the report. The individual who developed the proposal opportunity should be an important part of the team, since that person likely has the most contact with the recipient(s) of the proposal and may offer invaluable advice about how to approach various problems. If you have the opportunity to use someone from your public relations, communications, or advertising department on your proposal team, do so. These people are accustomed to deadline pressures and the mechanics of editing, typesetting or word processing, graphics, printing, collating, and binding. If such a person is not available to you, assign one person to handle those functions and allow enough time to do the job properly.

Deadlines

Obviously the proposal must be issued at some point, and that end point is the beginning of the planning as far as deadlines are concerned. Start with the issue date and work backward. Make a list of all the things that must be done, by function, and establish a date for completion of each. Make sure you allow enough time for each step, because you can be sure some deadlines will be missed along the way, and you will need to make up the time elsewhere. The people at the end of the production chain, such as printers, typesetters, word processing operators, etc., are accustomed to making up for time lost, but there is a limit to what people and machines can do. Your project may be just one of many rush jobs in word processing that day.

It is a good idea to schedule meetings at key points along the way to review the progress to make sure each team member is meeting the established deadlines. Such checkpoints might include the following.

1. The end of the information gathering stage.
2. The first draft review stage. Circulate copies prior to the meeting and ask team members to be prepared to comment on the draft at the meeting.
3. The final draft review stage. Copies reviewed prior to this meeting should include suggestions and corrections made on the first draft. This meeting should be for final polishing and approval only.

One final word about deadlines. If any deadlines are going to be missed that will affect the entire schedule, call a special meeting of the proposal team. Everybody hates surprises when they cause problems, and getting the team together may result in a solution to the problem and getting the proposal back on schedule. If your team is relatively inexperienced in producing proposals, you may want to schedule more frequent meetings to check the progress of the effort.

GENERAL CLASSIFICATIONS OF INTEROFFICE PROPOSALS

What should be included in the proposal may vary from situation to situation, but after your strategy session you should know precisely what the approach or theme of your proposal is going to be, and you should have a good idea of what should be included.

The elements to be included will be governed by the ultimate goal of the proposal. In interoffice proposals there are two principal types: proposals selling services to other groups within the organization and proposals seeking approval and funding. Most internal proposals are one or a combination of these.

Proposals Seeking Approval and Funding

Most large organizations get many people involved in the decision-making process to make sure the benefit of all the combined intelligence and expertise available is brought to bear to ensure success. To involve many people in the process means that copies must be distributed to the decision makers before they meet to discuss the alternatives. Your proposal is the vehicle through which you tell your story to that audience.

The formality of the proposal may depend on the formality of the company and the size and scope of what you are proposing. If you are suggesting a project that requires an expenditure of millions of dollars, a handwritten note on your memo paper may not suffice. On the other hand, your company may choose to limit the paperwork whenever possible and insist all proposals be limited to a few pages. Special situations are judgment calls that you must make based on your experience and knowledge of the company and its style of management.

As a general rule all proposals will require an explanation of what you are proposing, how you plan to accomplish it, what the benefits are to the company, and how much it will cost. The amount and depth of information you need to tell the story will depend on how large and how complex each of these elements is.

Examples of interoffice proposals seeking approval and funding might include purchase or lease of equipment, physical facilities, vehicles, advertising or public relations campaigns, engineering or marketing studies, or the publication of books.

Proposals Selling Services to Others in the Organization

The reasons for selling services to others within the organization may be equally diverse. You may be attempting to centralize certain functions for cost savings or efficiency. Or you may be attempting to amortize the cost of providing support services over a broader group. Whatever the reason, you are convinced that you need the enthusiastic support of the group you are proposing the idea to, or you would not be issuing a proposal.

You may be convinced that centralizing the data processing function, for example, will allow you to purchase more sophisticated hardware, employ more experienced data processing professionals, and save the company thousands of dollars in the process. Your task now is to convince the far-flung operating managers that they will benefit from this service and that they should either phase out their own systems or go on line with the central location.

Some of the managers may not be convinced quite so easily. After all, they may have made the initial decision to install the equipment they currently have, and you are now challenging the wisdom of that decision. Or the manager may view this as just another corporate boondoggle that is sure to raise his overhead allocation.

How do you convince this doubter? It is hoped that this question was addressed and an approach to the problem adopted in the planning phases, when you developed a strategy. By looking at the problem from his point of view, you have determined that in order to persuade him, you need to address certain issues:

- *Cost.* In any proposal cost is a consideration. A finite amount of money is available, and everyone would like more.
- *People.* Again, there is some limit on the amount of human resources available, and almost everyone needs more help. In this instance there is another personnel element. You may be displacing some of his employees if your project is approved.
- *Technology.* This element permeates many aspects of work today, especially in the data processing field. How do you assure your potential service user that you can provide state-of-the-art technology?
- *Service.* You are asking this manager to depend on you to provide the data needed, when it is needed, and in the configuration desired. The manager needs to be assured that you have the resources and management ability to make that happen.

How do these problems and considerations translate into the elements of a successful proposal? First and foremost, the theme of the report should address these considerations throughout the document, and, second, each piece of the proposal should play a role in answering his questions and objections. Let's review the elements.

ELEMENTS OF A PROPOSAL

Transmittal Memo

Every proposal of substance should have a transmittal memo, if for no other reason than to say, "Here is the proposal I promised you." If you use the transmittal memo to its fullest advantage, however, it is possible to accomplish much more.

The transmittal memo should set the stage for what you are about to present to your reader. It should tell him why you are issuing the proposal and call his attention to key portions or otherwise identify information that might be of interest specifically to him.

You should also point out any conditions governing the proposal, such as time constraints or adjustments in budgets or fees. In the data processing example, for instance, your proposal may be based on the current cost of computer equipment, and prices may be subject to change if action is not taken by a certain date.

The transmittal memo should also identify the next step. You may end the memo by saying; "I will telephone you next week to set up an appointment to discuss your reaction to this proposal." If you are really sure of yourself, or if you are unable to talk over the project with the recipient, you may end your memo with: "If, after reviewing the proposal, you agree with my recommendations, please sign the enclosed service agreement so we can place the order for the necessary equipment and begin implementation of our plan."

Table of Contents

There are no hard and fast rules about when to include a table of contents, but if your proposal is going to be ten pages or longer, it is a good idea to include one. Its purpose is not only to make it convenient for the reader to find various sections of the proposal but also to influence the reader positively by listing the elements that comprise your approach to the project.

Make sure it is neat, orderly, and descriptive. The table of contents should be the last part of the document prepared in order to make sure that it is accurate and that the pagination is correct.

List of Tables and Illustrations

Depending on the number of illustrations, charts, graphs, tables, etc., that you use, you may want to include a listing to help your reader find them quickly. Most readers like illustrations because they allow them to get the big picture without plowing through pages and pages of narrative. Help your reader out. Tell him up front where the illustrations are.

If you have only an illustration or two, and the report is relatively short, you may decide not to make a list, or you might decide to incorporate the location of the illustrations or tables into the table of contents. Purists would probably frown on such a suggestion, but the intent of the proposal is to sell something— an idea or a project—and there are no purists if the proposal is successful.

Executive Summary

On any proposal team there is always one person who counsels against including an executive summary or digest. The argument is that, if you include a summary, the recipient will not read the whole proposal. In actual fact, however, the only person who will probably read the entire proposal is the writer. Different people may read different sections that interest them and scan the portions they consider to be of lesser importance.

The idea is to make it as easy as possible for your reader. The executive summary allows the reader to get a feel for your approach before reading the entire document and to identify the sections that he would like to know more about before making a decision about your proposal.

As the saying goes, the benefit from including an executive summary is far greater than the risk of not including it.

The length of the summary may vary according to the situation at hand. Some proposal writers insist that it should never be more than one page in length, while others simply advise that you keep it short. My rule of thumb is to make the summary no more than one tenth of the length of the finished document and never more than four pages long. A twenty-page proposal would have a two-page summary and so on.

An executive summary should not be confused with an abstract. An abstract should be a condensed representation of the entire proposal, while an executive summary is not bound by any constraints other than to make it easy for the reader. As writer of the proposal, what you include in the executive summary is your option. Include the information you believe will be helpful in understanding the proposal and its approach, arranged and written in a manner that persuades the reader to take the action you would like.

Introduction

If there is a single most important function for the introduction to perform, it is to get all the readers to the same point of departure.

In the introduction you should identify the scope of the project, outline your approach to it, and state why you believe this is the best approach. If there are problems or limitations inherent in the project, they should also be identified and commented on in the introduction.

The introduction also provides a vehicle through which to call attention to the organization of the proposal, to particular sections, and to key elements within those sections. In short, the introduction tells the reader how you were thinking when you wrote the proposal so he can identify with your approach.

Other elements that you may wish to include in the introduction might be comments on why you are submitting the proposal and observations you made about the project during the course of your research.

If you do not use a transmittal memo, include a close in the introduction that calls for action. Identify what you plan to do and when; then ask the reader for a commitment. Even if you do include a similar paragraph in your transmittal memo, it is not a bad idea to summarize it again in the introduction to reinforce your previous statement or in the event that the transmittal memo gets separated from the proposal somewhere along the way.

Text or Body of the Proposal

The text or body of the proposal, as in a report, is where the sale is made or lost. The information you include in the body of the proposal should be so informative and so persuasive that your reader is led to the logical conclusion that your proposal should be adopted.

To ensure such success requires careful attention to the type and amount of information to include. The best guideline to follow is to make it easy for the reader. In the data processing example, for instance, if you think that a thorough technical explanation is necessary to convince potential users, then include it. If you think a short synopsis in layman's language in the text and a detailed explanation in the appendix is better, use them. You and your strategy team should identify those characteristics in your potential audience and make sure the proposal compensates for them.

The information included in the text of the proposal should be aimed at one of the general areas of cost, people, technology, and service. The material could probably be presented in any order, but, typically, the information necessary to make an informed decision is presented first, with costs, fees, and budgets last. In the data processing example the information could best be presented in the following order.

1. *Technology.* In this section you should address equipment necessary to perform the functions you are proposing and, if appropriate, give a comparison of models that best suit the needs of the firm. If various branches of the operation will be on line with a central computer, include information about the remote units and special features that may appeal to the users. If software packages are necessary to run the programs successfully, discuss them and their purpose. You would probably include flow charts to detail the storage and flow of information in this section as well.

2. *People.* Here is your opportunity to let your department shine. Talk about the expertise of your people and give examples in some detail of successful related projects you have undertaken in the past. Make sure you write to your readers in this situation. Relate the experience you have had to the problem at hand.

Include in this section information about how you plan to manage the project and present a schedule for the completion of the work. Plan to include the users in reviewing progress of the project, if possible, and identify checkpoints where users approve the progress to date before proceeding further.

Refer your readers to the appendix for resumes of key members of the project group, which detail their expertise in the field.

3. *Service.* In any project the users of the service want to make sure their needs are provided for, but in a situation such as that of our example, where an ongoing relationship is about to be established, service is especially important.

In this section you may decide to include some commentary about the philosophy of the company and your department. You might state that you view the division managers as important clients of your group, that you will stand or fail on your success with them, and that you emphatically intend to succeed.

Determination, and client service orientation, however noble, are not enough. Your users need to know the details of your service plan. What happens if their on-line unit breaks down just as they are about to transmit the month's financials? Your inclusion of a carefully thought out service plan with plenty of allowances for problems and contingencies will go a long way in this area.

4. *Costs.* Finally, the bottom line. In this section, include an estimate not only of the purchase price of the hardware or machinery but also of software costs (if applicable), travel expenses, installation charges, consulting fees, start-up costs, any additional personnel expenses, and ongoing costs such as those of service contracts, supplies, etc.

Be realistic with your numbers. Nothing will turn off a potential user more quickly than your trying to fool him about costs. If you can't justify the purchase on the basis of cost, emphasize the increased capability or better service, but don't try to make him believe you can do something that a knowledgeable person might find doubtful. He may talk to another expert who will poke holes in your argument, and if you use questionable numbers, you will never win over that potential user.

Break down the costs in every way the reader might. If your numbers are difficult to understand, you will only frustrate your audience. Again, make it easy for the reader.

Exhibits and Appendices

The purpose of an appendix or exhibit section of a proposal is to include information that may be related to the topic of the proposal but is too detailed, lengthy, or otherwise unwieldy to include in the text. Examples might be resumes of project staffers, related articles or brochures, detailed technical or financial computations, technical data, or other related tables used in computing prices or fees that you included elsewhere in the proposal.

As you write the text portion of the proposal, make a list of the supporting information you used, to consider later for possible inclusion in the appendix section. If there is any doubt when you are writing the proposal as to whether a certain table should be included as a table or figure in the text or included in the appendix, put it in the back. If it was sufficiently detailed to cause you to wonder, it probably belongs in the appendix.

9

Types of Proposals and Uses of Each

"I am the world's greatest salesman; therefore I must make it easy for people to buy."

F. W. Woolworth

What you are selling will, of course, influence more than anything else the type and style of proposal you select. After you have decided on the best approach to sell your idea it is time to select the vehicle that will best deliver that approach.

If the project has been discussed and generally agreed on before being committed to writing, a simple confirming letter may suffice. If you are proposing a project that will require substantial funding, and several people with different levels of knowledge will be involved in making the decision, no doubt you will need a more comprehensive proposal.

The type of activity you are proposing will also influence your selection of the vehicle to deliver your idea. If you provide a service to others in the company on a regular basis, and the firm has a policy for interoffice charges for those services, you may decide to develop a standardized proposal for which you can "fill in the blanks" as needed. The purpose of such a proposal would be to spell out the terms and conditions of the agreement and make sure that everyone involved has the same understanding of the project.

Interoffice proposals are generally divided into four basic types, depending on their length and purpose:

- *Proposal letter or memorandum.* The proposal letter may simply confirm and formalize an agreement reached earlier, or it may be a stand-alone proposal for a project that is neither complex nor expensive enough to warrant a longer document.
- *Standardized proposals.* Standardized proposals might be used in service areas such as advertising or communications or in technical areas such as engineering or research and development. Funding proposals may include standardized capital equipment requests and standard operating unit business plans. Standardized proposals may vary in length from very short to very long.
- *Short proposals.* Generally fairly informal in appearance and content, short proposals differ from standardized proposals not only in length but also in that they are developed for a specific purpose and are written for such a one-time use. How short is short? It's an arbitrary call, but as for reports, if a proposal and all its attachments, exhibits, and so forth amount to ten pages or less, it would generally be considered short.
- *Formal proposals.* The formal proposal is longer, more comprehensive, and usually has most or all of the traditional elements associated with proposals, including a detailed, persuasive narrative aimed at selling a major project.

Let's review the elements of each of the types of proposals identified and look at some examples.

PROPOSAL LETTER

The proposal letter may be individually addressed and typed if the project is large and the group receiving it is small, or it may be a form letter or memo if the distribution prohibits the production of individual letters.

Generally a proposal letter would be no longer than three or four pages; two would be ideal. Nevertheless, every proposal letter, regardless of length, should address the four basic issues:

(1) people, (2) technology (if appropriate), (3) service, and (4) cost.

Below is an example of a letter proposal distributed to the 200-plus members of the governing council of the Professional Photographers of America, Inc. It was duplicated and distributed in memo form because of the size of the audience.

April 15, 19xx

To: National Council

From: Bob Becker

Subject: Winona proposal

The Board of Directors and the Winona Trustees propose that the Winona School of Professional Photography be relocated to our headquarters in Des Plaines, Illinois. The proposal is the result of careful study and thought. Please review the following facts:

For more than 60 years, PP of A (Professional Photographers of America, Inc.) has recognized the need for continuing education of the professional photographer. Education continues to be the backbone of the services offered by our organization.

Continuing education is provided by the PP of A in many ways, including conventions, The Professional Photographer magazine, newsletters, and seminars. Our main thrust, however, has been the Winona School of Professional Photography.

Our Society owes the Daguerre Club of Indiana a permanent debt of gratitude for launching our national continuing education effort by providing a facility that has lasted us 60 years. The school has been a success and continues to be a success. More than 27,000 photographers have come to Winona Lake since 1922 in order to update skills or explore new facets of the profession. They have worked with a faculty of successful professionals willing to share their experience, knowledge, and techniques in specialized areas.

We must, nevertheless, face the problems the school is encountering. In order to obtain an objective analysis of our existing problem, the Winona Trustees, with the approval of PP of A Board of Directors, engaged a consulting firm to review the school's needs, to inspect the facilities, to analyze the student population, to establish criteria for an ideal location, and to recommend future direction.

Our consultants reached the following conclusions:

1. It would cost more than $1 million to update the Winona Lake facilities. (Adjust that figure to $1,150,000 in 19xx.)

2. The Winona Lake Location is no longer practical.

    a. Attendance has reached a plateau.
    b. Airline service into the nearest airport, Fort Wayne, is limited. International students fly to O'Hare, then must drive at least three hours to reach the school. A school with international appeal needs to be accessible by air.
    c. The Winona area is not serviced by interstate highways, making automobile travel tedious, even for students who drive to the school.
    d. A school isolated and distant from headquarters is difficult to administer and maintain.

3. St. Louis measured best and the Chicago area measured second best, when considering international air service, wage differentials, cost of living, overall state business climate, cost of new construction, and proximity to PP of A membership. The consultants reached this conclusion after thoroughly analyzing the 50 largest air hubs for potential locations for the school.

4. Cost and convenience to students made Des Plaines a first choice.

    a. The cost to move and build in a new location outside Chicago would be $3,089,052. (Adjust for inflation to $3,540,000 for 19xx.)
    b. The cost to move and build in a new

Chicago area site would be $2,882,310.
(Adjust for inflation to $3,300,000
for 19xx.)

c.   The cost of consolidating on the present
Des Plaines site is $1,775,000.   (Ad-
just for inflation to $2,000,000 for
19xx.)

5.   Since we already own land in Des Plaines,
and since Des Plaines is a healthy, viable
business community with one of the best
real estate tax bases in the Chicago area,
and since we are near moderately priced
motels, a Forest Preserve system (excellent
resource for on-location photography)
and O'Hare International Airport, we
recommend that Winona School of Professional Photography be brought home to Des
Plaines.

A slide presentation detailing cost specifics and
all the ramifications of the proposed move will be
presented at the Council meeting at our annual convention in July in Las Vegas.   At that time the
Board will formally request approval from Council,
and the proposal will be submitted for a vote.
Please plan to attend the meeting.

STANDARDIZED PROPOSAL

Despite its description, the standardized proposal usually
changes slightly to accommodate minor variations on the same
theme. The layout, the headings, and the general elements included are the same, but the number of points under each may
vary, depending on the size and scope of the project.

If the terms and conditions and the activity being performed
are similar, a proposal is ideal for standardization. An example of
a proposal used by the design department of a large manufacturing firm to identify the tasks to be performed in the project and to
clarify the interoffice billing arrangements follows. Since this is a
one-time project with little need for ongoing service, and the
people in the design group are well known to their intercompany
clientele, this standardized proposal emphasizes the services to be
performed in the course of the project, the budget, and the terms
of the agreement. The technology portion of the proposal is
inherent in the product itself.

DESIGN PROPOSAL

To: H. Hogan   January 21, 19xx
         Los Angeles

From: L. Radtke
         Silicon Valley

Projects: Appearance design of the following prod-
          ucts for the Automotive Division

          ● Digital scope analyzer
          ● Digital scope emission analyzer
          ● Portable stand for emission analyzer

Design Factors:

     1. Use existing scope molded case.
     2. Design upper housing to fit existing
         base, but to look different than
         present model.
     3. Housing should accommodate scope
         analyzer and emission analyzer.
     4. Consider red color case.
     5. Consider common chassis for both
         models.
     6. Incorporate all components and
         switches per engineering specifica-
         tions.
     7. Design the portable stand to
         accommodate both models.

Stage I--Conceptual Design

     Design recommendations will be made in the
form of:

          ● Preliminary scale details showing
            front, side, and top views.
          ● Colored perspective drawings.
          ● Preliminary full-size detail of
            alternative control panel layouts.
          ● A meeting of the design review group
            to conclude this stage.

                         Stage I Budget $5,000

Stage IA--Conceptual Design, Portable Stand

          ● Preliminary scale detail drawings.

- Colored perspective sketches.
- Presented at Design review meeting Stage I.

Stage IA Budget $3,000

Stage II--Design Finalization

Incorporating the desired features of Stage I design suggestions, the Design Department will prepare the following:

- Final detailed drawing of upper housing.
- Two final detailed drawings of front control panels (both models).
- Full-size colored composite of front control panel with overlay for alternate model, using actual type style, sizes, and colors.

Stage II Budget $8,000

Stage III--Artwork

Following approval of the design, if desired, the following services will be provided by the Design Department upon completion of Stage II:

- Camera-ready artwork for control panels
- Prototype models of upper housing
- Prototype model of protable stand

Stage III Budget $3,000

Out-of-Pocket Expenses

We expect that out-of-pocket expenses for this project will be minimal and limited to purchases of typesetting, photostats, messenger service, and specialized illustrations from outside suppliers. In addition, there may be some modest travel expense involved to attend meetings with the engineering department and others involved in the project.

Expense budget $2,000

The Working Agreement

The Design Department will open a contract on

this project to which our time and expenses will be charged. Upon conclusion of the project we will initiate an interoffice charge memorandum to have the charges allocated to your Division.

Any charges other than those outlined in this proposal must be approved by you in advance and will be charged back to the Division at cost.

We will begin work immediately upon receipt of your approval indicated by your signature below.

Total Budget $21,000

Approved By

_____
Design Department

_____
Automotive Division

_____
Date

Short Proposal

The short proposal incorporates more of the elements of a formal proposal than either the letter or the standard proposal. The inclusion of a table of contents, introduction, and appendix, however, may not be necessary when the topic being discussed is relatively simple and inexpensive according to company standards.

If the scope of the project is substantial, but not large enough to be considered major, the short proposal is probably ideal.

Leasing proposals, capital equipment requests, small advertising and public relations campaigns, and book, newsletter, or brochure publication proposals might be good examples of projects that would be suited for short proposals.

It is a good idea to outline a short proposal if it is going to be at least five to ten pages in length. In shorter versions a list of the elements to be covered should be sufficient as a guide to make sure all the elements you planned to include actually are there.

FORMAL PROPOSAL

The formal proposal should always be outlined before writing it in order to make sure that the elements you planned to include are all there and that the amount of time and space you spend on each is in accordance with its relative importance to the entire proposal.

In your proposal team strategy session you should identify the key elements of the proposal and develop an approach to writing it, but you may want to go a step further and complete an outline for all to review and approve before beginning the drafting of the proposal. Whether or not the group reviews the outline, you should develop one for your own use. (For outlining assistance, refer to Chapter 4.)

Examples of a formal proposal might include a lengthy non-standard business plan, an extensive advertising campaign, a request for funding for a research or market development project, approval of a construction project, or a proposed acquisition of another company.

The rest of this chapter is a sample proposal for an advertising campaign for a newly opened branch bank in a high-rise office complex. The purpose of the proposal was to get funding and approval for the plan. It was written by Thomas L. Marin, now head of his own advertising agency in Chicago.

Portions of the actual proposal were shortened, and exhibits were omitted for space considerations in this example. In an actual proposal, however, items to be included in exhibits might be marketing research studies, media schedules, rate tables, and responsibilities of the advertising agency team and the internal advertising department. Accompanying the proposal might be layouts of sample advertisements, storyboards of proposed TV commercials, and scripts of radio spots (if the campaign called for both broadcast and print advertising).

<u>Memo</u>

To: T. J. McGlone   Date: April 27, 19xx

From: T. L. Marin

Subject: Branch Facility Marketing Approach

    Attached, for your review, is a proposal
outlining our suggested approach to marketing
banking services at the branch facility.

    We have identified key target markets we
believe to be the most likely customers of the
bank and developed an approach to marketing selected
services of each.

    Both my staff and I are enthusiastic about
the opportunity to work on this exciting project
and are ready to begin immediately upon approval
of the proposal.

    I will telephone you next week to schedule an
appointment to discuss details of the project, its
funding, the role of the corporate advertising
department and branch facility's management to
ensure the success of this marketing program.

    We look forward to being a part of the
facility's business development team in this new
venture.

A New
Marketing
Approach

Prepared by:

Thomas Marin

TABLE OF CONTENTS

EXECUTIVE SUMMARY

It is no secret that the banking industry is becoming increasingly competitive. If we are to ensure the success of our new branch facility in the Metro Center Complex, we must develop a carefully thought out marketing strategy supported by the advertising and public relations efforts necessary to make it work.

We suggest that our efforts be directed to four key markets:

- Small business. In marketing Metro Center Bank (MCB) to this audience we will emphasize a theme similar to "Your banker should be your friend," to let small business owners know we offer the kind of friendly service and financial advice they need and want.

- Executive investment. With this group of professionals earning over $25,000 per year, we will offer counseling and assistance with personal investments, tax shelters, all savers certificates, and the like.

- Secretarial force. Convenience and financial advice will be the emphasis

in our campaign to attract secretaries
as customers of MCB.

- <u>Service industry</u>. We will target our
efforts to professionals in the
advertising, accounting, consulting,
and architectural firms that lease
space in the complex.

For the first three audiences we will develop
advertising and public relations support around a
series of separate seminars designed to appeal to
each audience, then advertise them in the trade
papers that reach the audience we are attempting
to attract.

Public relations efforts will focus on
attendance promotion for the seminars, inviting
editors and writers to attend the meetings for
interviews and follow-up stories, and, in certain
instances where the likelihood of success seems
greatest, we will condense the seminar into an
article for placement in a national or regional
magazine to be reprinted and distributed locally.

For the fourth audience, the service industry,
our marketing will be more personal. We will
design and produce a desktop presentation and
related brochures that bank marketing representatives

can take to the prospective customer's office for a personal presentation.

Such a coordinated program, we are convinced, will firmly establish MCB as an important banking influence in the markets in which we have chosen to compete.

INTRODUCTION

The banking industry as a whole is competitive on both a personal and a commercial level and is becoming increasingly more competitive daily. Therefore, it is critically important for the Metro Center Bank (MCB) to develop a well-defined marketing plan that accurately focuses on potential customers and strategically implements a program to attract this clientele.

The purpose of this plan is to identify the potential customers of our facility that is located in the complex and to recommend promotion methods that will effectively attract their business.

SITUATION ANALYSIS

Based upon MCB's experience with commercial businesses and personal investments, and its ability to adapt to changing business trends and attitudes, we have a tremendous potential for increased sales through the facility at Metro Center.

Because of our solid reputation with, and the significant amount of experience we have with, small to medium-sized companies, it is our con- clusion that a marketing plan directed toward smaller companies offers MCB the greatest potential for growth.

Our medium size is an advantage. It will allow us to position the facility as banking experts for smaller businesses while providing a high ceiling for personal investments and deposits.

On the negative side, located in Metro Center is a direct competitor--The Downtown Bank. Offering similar banking services and conveniences, it poses a real threat to the facility's growth. Also, there are other banks located in the area, such as the Commercial Bank and the State Bank, that are significant competitors of the facility. Simply emphasizing our all-purpose theme and being conveniently located is not going to be enough to achieve the sales objectives facility management desires. We believe it is essential that MCB demonstrates its commitment by providing a program that is helpful to the customers we are attempting to attract. It is apparent that convenience is a primary factor in the selection of a bank. Therefore, with competitive banks also located in Metro Center, it is essential that we offer real services such as this program defines.

KEY MARKETS

We recommend separating the following prospective clients into separate audiences and selling to them as individual markets, as opposed to mass advertising. The four audiences with the most potential are:

1) Small Business ($5 million or less in annual sales)
2) Executive Investment
3) Secretarial Force
4) Service Industry

Small Business

In a recent report from the Small Business Administration it was noted that presidents, chief financial officers, and principals of small businesses are more concerned with establishing a

long-term, personal relationship with their bank
than they are with the actual services offered.
These businessmen want to meet their banker and
discuss business, obtain financial advice, and
learn of innovative banking services. "Your banker
should be your friend" is a theme that could be
used to promote the facility's personalized banking
service for small businessmen.

Executive Investment

Executives earning $25,000 and more are keenly
interested in personal investments, tax shelters,
all savers certificates, custodian accounts, and
similar services. They are more informed than
yesterday's investors and are interested in receiving quality advice from their banker. Our program
will provide an environment for executives to feel
comfortable in, one that will result in a trusting
relationship with their bank counselor.

It is important to note that many executives,
in addition to their principal employer, have an
investment in or can otherwise influence other
businesses and that personal banking relationships
often develop into commercial accounts with those
other businesses.

Secretarial Force

Convenience and financial advice are the two

key attributes secretaries look for in their banks.
With hundreds of secretaries working in Metro
Center the potential for their business is substan-
tial.

Service Industry

Today MCB serves a great number of advertising
agencies. We can capitalize on this experience
and use it in our promotion to both new and
established agencies. Banking convenience and
industry experience can go a long way with prospective agencies, particularly if there is dissatisfaction with their present banking relationship.

In addition to agencies, there are many types
of service-related companies with high-paid
executives and professionals located in Metro Center.
Some of those who lease space in the center include
public relations agencies, architects, accounting
and consulting firms. They are excellent prospects
for the facility and offer an opportunity to expand
our business significantly.

ADVERTISING AND PUBLIC RELATIONS SUPPORT

The primary purpose of this advertising and
public relations program is to provide an overall
awareness of the facility in Metro Center and to
create a favorable atmosphere for a "Calling
Officer" of the bank. We will position the facility

as the businessperson's personal account manager
by stressing the general message "We care."

Trying to be clever or cute has no place in
this marketing plan. Research has proven that puns
and cliches are not effective, at best, and are
sometimes counterproductive in the promotion of a
bank's services. There are plenty of real advantages available to promote the facility.

All literature, trade ads, signage, and
seminars will emphasize MCB's experience and
commitment to the downtown area and will be consistent in both message and design.

We anticipate that a modest amount of public
relations support will enhance our overall efforts,
particularly in promotion of the seminars outlined
later in this proposal.

THE PLAN

Small Business

A. Collateral Program

After reviewing the literature that is
currently available, we came to believe
that a more modern approach should be
taken to properly reflect the facility's
image in today's business environment.
Also, the current literature does not

seem to reflect a consistent theme in its message or design. We recommend producing new materials that will identify MCB's services and substantiate our commitment to the business community. A generic "Sell the Bank" piece aimed at small businesses is needed. Individual service booklets should also be designed, using a family resemblance. The message "We Care," with a family design resemblance, will be stressed in all materials we produce.

B. Signage

Improved signage in the facility, advertising the services of the bank, will be produced, drawing from the design of the collateral program.

C. Media

Trade and business section advertising in publications that reach our audience will be used to announce individual events. A trade ad with a return coupon could ilustrate a roomful of sleeping seminar attendees and pose the question "Are you tired of boring seminars?" The copy would request the reader's preference of banking and investment seminar subjects and that he mail his ideas to MCB.

D. Seminars

Seminars will be held in Metro Center. The audience will be current facility customers and business associates. We will send written invitations through the mail to presidents and chief financial officers of target companies and feature keynote speakers at lunch meetings. The marketing emphasis will be: a satisfied customer produces referrals and new customers. Seminar topics will be designed around the responses from our trade ads in C (above).

E. Public Relations

The thrust of the public relations efforts will be to provide feature stories to financial editors of the metropolitan media regarding MCB's commitment to small business, using the copy theme, "Big Bank Woos Small Business!" We will keep editors and writers informed of seminars and invite them to attend. If they do attend the meetings, we will attempt to interest writers and editors in interview-

ing speakers and bank officers to supplement
features they may write.

Executive Investment

A. Collateral Program
Individual booklets can be used that will
be developed for the small business
audience.

B. Media
Trade ads will be scheduled to run in
business publications, announcing the
seminar's dates and subject matter. They
should be similar in format to the small
business trade ad to reinforce general
awareness and our commitment to the business
community.

C. Seminars
The emphasis is on investors. Seminar
programs will be delivered by bank
officers, investment brokers, and
financial consultants. Admission is
free, and refreshments will be offered.

D. Public Relations
An ongoing press release effort will be
maintained to inform the metropolitan
media and its readers about seminars, as
well as to invite the press to cover the

events, and we will arrange interviews
with our speakers and officers whenever
possible. We will extend invitations to a
selected list of speakers from our target
audience of investors.

Secretarial Force

A. Announcements

Flyers will be prepared and distributed
at lunchtime in Metro Center buildings
regarding the facility's services and
seminar dates.

B. Signage

Signs will be produced announcing bank
services and seminars in the lobby of the
Metro Center Facility.

C. Media

Trade ads announcing seminar dates and
subject matter will be scheduled to run in
publications that reach this group.
Subjects to be stressed would be coordinated
with the seminar topic selected.

D. Seminars

"How to manage your money" might be a theme
for a secretarial seminar. An informal
lunch with a personal bank counselor and
officer is recommended to make the event

pleasant and comfortable. Women who own
their own businesses would be good choices
for alternative speakers or in conjunction
with our own speakers.

E. Public Relations

We will concentrate our efforts on
publications that appeal to working
women. In addition to publicizing the
seminars to local writers and editors, we
will attempt to develop a feature article
(based on seminar presentations) for
placement in a national or regional
magazine for working women. If we are
successful, we will reprint the article
for local distribution.

Service Industry

A. Executive Presentation/Desktop

We will produce a service-related industry
brochure and a flip chart presentation to
dramatically present MCB's services. A
flip chart will allow a bank representative
to select the appropriate subject for each
company executive he calls on. An interesting, informative, service-related brochure
that identifies the various service
companies MCB has experience with, and

the services offered, will be produced.

B. Personal Solicitation

We believe that personal solicitation of
the service industry professionals supported by attractive and informative
collateral materials can produce a
significant amount of new business for
the facility.

Summary

The four markets of small business, executive
investment, secretarial, and service industry
represent a long-term profit opportunity for MCB.
Our marketing plan positions the facility at Metro
Center on a strong foundation both now and for the
future.

MCB has an opportunity to increase its market
share significantly in 1982 and become a dominant
banking influence in the proposed markets.

BUDGETS

Space Cost

Six b/w 3 col. x 10 in.

newspaper advertise-

ments @ $1,650 ea......... $ 9,900

Six b/w 7x10 magazine ads

@ $910 ea................. 5,460

Six b/w 7x10 specialty

publication ads @

$374 ea.................... 2,244

Total Space Cost........ $17,604

Production Cost

Preparation of three b/w

7x10 advertisements @

$600 ea.................... $ 1,800

Total Production Cost... $ 1,800

Collateral Materials

Eight-page small business

brochure................... $ 3,000

Six-page service brochure...... $ 2,500

Four booklets on bank

services @ $1,000 ea...... $ 4,000

Ten-page flip chart for

service industry.......... $ 2,500

Four signs for lobby @

$250 ea........................ $ 1,000

Total Collateral Cost............ $13,000

Agency Fees

Pro rata share of advertising and

relations firms' retainers

($500 monthly for six

months)................... $ 3,000

Total Agency Fees.......... $ 3,000

Seminars

    Room rentals; 3 [$250 ea...... $ 750

    Food, coffee, and soft drinks

        based on an attendance

        of 100 people per seminar..$ 1,200

    Production of handout

        materials and audiovisual

        support.................. $ 1,000

        Total Seminar Cost...... $ 2,950

        Budget Grand Total...... $38,354

ACTION PLAN

Upon approval of this proposal, the Advertising Department will meet with MCB officers to establish timetables and agree on an implementation strategy. After plans and deadlines are in place we will begin working on creative concepts for our promotion theme to be followed throughout the campaign.

Each phase of the plan will be subject to review and approval by MCB officers before proceeding to the next step in the process. Such approvals will ensure that the marketing strategy complements the bank's overall business plan and that costs are carefully monitored.

Such teamwork, we are confident, will greatly assist in the implementation of a highly successful program to attract and retain MCB customers.

10

Proposals—How to Approach the Project

*"Successful salesmanship is 90 percent preparation
and 10 percent presentation."*
                                                    Bertrand R. Canfield

A successful proposal, like a successful report, requires extensive preparation. If you are to persuade others to purchase your
services or fund your project, you must first understand the
problem or situation so thoroughly yourself that you can lead the
reader easily to the same logical conclusion that you reached.

If you are not yourself persuaded that the alternative you are
proposing is the best one for the company and everyone involved
in the project, you are not ready to write the proposal.

The information-gathering phase of proposal writing is very
similar to the same phase in report writing. Companies that issue
comprehensive proposals to outside clients may spend thousands
of dollars and hundreds of man-hours determining precisely the
scope of the problem that the proposal is offering a solution to
and direct every word in the report toward solving that problem.

While internal proposals may not be quite so elaborate, the
approach to them is essentially the same. Because you are a part
of the company, you already have a good understanding of how it
operates, how key people respond to various problem-solving
approaches, and what the general firm policies are.

If you are unfamiliar with policies, the company's employee handbook, management guide, or other similar references should provide information about approval policies. Other people who have successfully submitted similar proposals are valuable resources as well. Talk to them and determine why their proposals were successful.

If possible, review your planned proposal with its key recipients. Use a little salesmanship. Tell them you have an idea that you think will save the company a lot of money, expand the business, or improve the operating efficiency and that you want to make sure that the idea is presented to them in a way that is most convenient and useful for them.

If it is not possible to speak directly to the recipients, and you cannot locate anyone else in the company who has prepared a similar successful proposal (with whom you can talk face to face), try to locate copies of proposals that you can read and extract ideas from. If your company doesn't have a central source for storing and retrieving such information, circulate a memo to those you think might have useful information or put a notice in your employee publication asking anyone with information that might be of value to get in touch with you.

Of course, this presumes that you have enough time to do these things, and very often deadlines are so short that such luxuries are not available. If you are faced with a situation in which there is no information readily available, and no time to spend gathering it, spend the thinking time that you do have available looking at the situation from the point of view of the person or people who must approve your proposal.

If you were in that person's position, what sort of information would you insist on before making this decision? What information would you like to have in addition to the essential information? What kind of constraints would you have because of your responsibilities to others? Will this project influence your life in any way? Will it solve problems or create them?

PROPOSING A NEW PROJECT

If you are proposing a new concept or something your company has never done before, certain areas require more attention than they would in projects that are more or less ongoing parts of the company's operations. To persuade the decision makers that they should approve your project, you should emphasize:

1. *Benefits to the company.* The best justification for funding a new project or selling a service is that it will make or save money. If that is the situation, you have a strong foundation. Often, however, the cost/benefit relationship is not quite so apparent. The project may have a big up-front cost and a long wait before profits or savings are actually realized. In that event, paint a truthful but optimistic picture of cost/benefit considerations but emphasize other things such as an improvement in efficiency or productivity, a competitive advantage, or an investment in the future. Whatever advantages you emphasize, the thrust of the proposal should be the benefit to the company as a whole, not to your department or another smaller special-interest group within the total organization.

2. *Minimal risk.* No one wants to be associated with a project that bombs. Make sure you have identified all the potential risks and addressed them in your proposal. Everything in business has a certain amount of risk, and decision makers are accustomed to taking chances. Before taking that chance, however, they want to make sure that a sensible plan is in place to deal with problems and contingencies. If you don't address the risks and tell your readers how you plan to deal with them, they can only assume that you did not plan for problems, or that you chose not to address them in the proposal. Neither alternative is as effective as meeting potential problems head-on with a well thought out plan for dealing with them as they arise and checkpoints at strategic points along the way to identify them before they become serious enough to impair the progress of the project.

3. *Project management and skills.* Even if the project is a radical departure from anything the company has ever done before, and it is risky in every way, it does not mean you cannot sell your services or fund your project. One element of the proposal that will assure your audience that the project will be successful is the portion that deals with the

people who will staff the project. If you have managed a similar or equally difficult project (in your present company or a previous one), use that as an example of how you made it work before. If you haven't, emphasize the skills and education you have that will aid you in this project. Include information about the rest of the project's staffers and their qualifications for working on this proposed project and insuring its success.

4. *Your implementation plan.* Provide details of how you plan to implement various phases of the plan after its approval. Include schedules of various elements of the project, the names of those responsible for managing those elements, and information on how they will be monitored to make sure the job gets done. If it is a big project that will require months or even years to complete, break it down into manageable pieces with a reporting and approval plan for each phase of the project. Include a separate reporting arrangement for exceptions and contingencies. Let the proposal approvers know that there is a system for providing information to management about serious problems that may cause lengthy delays in completion of the project.

In short, if you are proposing a new project, you are asking your company to take a chance that you will deliver what you've promised and that everyone will be better off for having done so. Your proposal should leave them no room for doubt. Your readers should be convinced that this is the thing to do.

PROPOSING A CONTINUING PROJECT

On the surface it may appear that proposing a continuing project might be easier than selling a totally new concept. Not necessarily. Your readers may be tired of the project and may be beginning to view it as a never-ending boondoggle that just keeps eating money. Even if they have no negative feelings about it, members of the board of directors and management charged with wise management of the company's resources are continually aware of that responsibility and must evaluate your proposal according to its overall value to the company.

Proposing a continuing project requires a slight shift in emphasis:

1. Recap the benefits already derived from the project. Use concrete examples of successes, whether they be in cost savings, profit improvements, new discoveries, image enhancement, or a competitive advantage. Just because the project is an ongoing one, don't assume it isn't necessary to sell it. True, you may not have to sell it as hard, but it should be sold continually to reassure the decision makers that they made the right decision when they approved the project in the first place. And some of the players may have changed either in the project management and staffing group or in the decision-making group. They may not be as familiar with the project as you think.

2. Include schedules met and yet to be met. Demonstrate the progress you have made already and show how the completed portions of the schedule relate to the entire project. Provide detailed schedules and affix responsibility for implementation of future portions of the project. For projects that require long periods of time to complete, emphasize the management controls that you have installed to make sure every element of the project is under control and on schedule.

3. Review savings to the company. If you saved money in any phase of the project or completed parts of the plan ahead of schedule, point to those examples of how well the project is going. If you have stayed within budget and finished certain portions slightly late because of problems, say so, but emphasize the things you did well.

4. Remind readers why you are involved. It probably isn't necessary to spend a lot of time on it, but remind your decision makers why the company initiated the project in the first place. If those reasons are still valid, tell them so; if you have since discovered even more compelling reasons why you should be involved, so much the better.

5. Divide the project into pieces. Make sure your plan includes all aspects of the project but divide it into manageable units that are building blocks for the entire project. Don't give the impression that you are asking for thousands or millions of

dollars to go out and develop something that you will bring back in a few months or years neatly wrapped with a ribbon around it. Show how the project will be completed in phases, with approvals at certain points along the way. Fix a final completion date so there is no doubt in the reader's mind when the project will be totally finished.

TAKING THE OFFENSIVE IN A PROPOSAL

All too often proposal writers give the impression that they hate to ask for the order or that, because they think the project is a good idea, everyone else should too. Unfortunately it doesn't always work that way. If you are proposing something, those you are proposing it to expect to be persuaded, and they expect to be told exactly what it is you want and how much it will cost. You may say you would rather discuss costs, for example, in person so you can go into greater detail and judge the reaction. That's fine if you can do it and if you are all thinking in the same general area of what it is likely to cost. But if you are thinking millions and your decision-making group is thinking thousands, all the meeting will do is embarrass everybody involved.

Tell the reader exactly what it is you want to do and what it is likely to cost. Be aggressive in your explanation of the benefits to the company and be positive about your request for funding. Take the initiative with your audience. It is your project, and you must sell it. No matter how many people may have been involved in the strategy development or project planning, the proposal writer must persuade the audience to approve the plan.

Take the offensive in your writing style as well. This does not mean that you should be abrasive or arrogant, but you should lead your readers in the direction you would like them to go. To quote an anonymous writer, "Tell the reader what you are going to tell him; tell him; then tell him what you've told him." That is good advice in any type of writing, but especially in business writing.

PUTTING UP YOUR DEFENSES

Unfortunately, life is not one success after another for most of us. We usually have a few failures along the way, and some of those failures may be remembered by the company's decision makers long after we have buried them in the back of our own minds.

If previous failures or problems are likely to influence the approval of your proposal negatively, they should be addressed. Simply pretending that the problems don't exist is no guarantee that your decision makers won't remember them. There is, of course, no pleasant way to deal with our own failures. We hate to admit failure even to ourselves—and especially to others.

If you are put in a position of defending a poor record—either yours or one of your project staffer's—address the issue positively. If you had a problem meeting deadlines in the past, for example, point out the controls you have installed in your plan to make sure everything is completed on schedule and build in more management checkpoints to reassure them that they will know about problems in advance and in time to do something about them. If your problem was cost overruns, talk cost controls.

Do not, however, belabor past problems. In fact, it is often better to allude to problems rather than mention them outright. This can be done by emphasizing the parts of the plan you have developed to eliminate those problems before they ever arise.

If your last new product introduction was a dud in the marketplace, talk about the ratio of failures to successes in new product introductions and remind your readers that it is a risky business, but identify the steps you have taken to minimize the risk—marketing research, test marketing, and expected demand, for example—and include a realistic timetable for a return on the company's investment in the new product.

UNDERSTANDING THE OBJECTIVES

The objectives vary from project to project, of course, but they also vary according to type of proposal. If you are writing a proposal seeking funding, you should be concerned more with the company's overall objectives and how your project fits into them.

If you are selling services to another group within the company, you should be more concerned with the objectives of that group and how your services are going to help them meet their sales or profit goals, or their new product design and development plan, and so on.

With modern management structures that emphasize participation by many levels of employees, we are almost all involved in selling our ideas to others, and to do so we must clearly understand what we are trying to sell and what the objectives of the recipient of our sales pitch are.

As illustrated in the formal proposal example in the previous chapter, a portion of the proposal should be used to define the objective or problem, the scope and size of the problem, and then to develop a plan to solve the problem or meet the objective. This statement of the objective should be included early in the proposal, either in the introduction or at the beginning of the proposal itself. If your objective or understanding of the problem is wrong, how far do you think you will get with your audience? Likewise, if your stated objective conflicts with management's goals, you will get about the same reaction from your readers.

The way to avoid that unpleasant experience is to make sure you understand the problem or objective clearly yourself and know how it relates to the company's overall goals and objectives.

METHODOLOGY TO BE USED

In a proposal selling services or a project that is service related, methodology is especially important, because the results are not as tangible and measurable as the physical construction or manufacture of something. Describing the methodology to be used would be an integral part of a proposal seeking funding for a marketing research project or a research and experimentation project.

Even if it is a more tangible project such as a new product, the methods you plan to use, such as market testing different package designs or pricing structures, will reassure your readers that your approach is sound and that financial risks have been minimized.

Proposals seeking funding for manufacturing projects might address the need for pilot plant operations to test the efficiency of one method over another before committing large amounts of capital to the construction of a new facility. A business plan would address all the things that the group or department plans for the next year and the methods it plans to employ to get the job done.

STAFFING THE PROJECT

The people assigned to the project are certainly an important consideration, whether you are seeking funding, selling services, or both. Management needs to be assured that you have the right people in sufficient numbers to ensure success.

Include an organization chart as a part of the proposal or in the appendix to help the readers get a firm fix on the lines of authority and who is responsible for what. If all the people assigned are not well known to the readers, include resumes. (For assistance in designing an effective proposal resume, see Chapter 11.)

Make sure you have the people with the right skills for this particular project and emphasize those skills. If there are people in the company who have a reputation for being exceptionally good in one area or another that you are involved in, enlist their aid as advisors to the project, even if their involvement is limited to a few phone calls and a review of the final report. Include their names in the proposal as advisors to give credibility to the project and to guarantee their interest in the successful conclusion of the project.

You may even want to include some of your critics as advisors. While this may be a small source of aggravation during the project, it may prevent them from trying to scuttle it, if they have an interest in its success by virtue of the fact that their names are associated with the project. And you may be surprised; they may make a positive contribution. They may have been critical in the past because they thought they could do the job better. Now, by adding them to the team, you are giving them a chance to show their stuff.

Make sure that you have planned to include enough people to staff the project. Include management, technical people, laborers, and any others who may be involved in your estimates; be certain that you make allowances for vacations, sick leaves, and down time; and remember that nobody is 100-percent productive. Give yourself a little cushion in your plan but calculate the amount of time and number of people needed to accomplish each aspect of the project and include that information in your staffing plan.

THE READER'S PARTICIPATION

The role of the proposal recipient in the project should be

clearly identified. If you are simply seeking approval for the project, and once the funding is assured the reader has no further responsibility, that should be apparent in either the close of the proposal or your transmittal letter or memo. If, on the other hand, your reader will have an ongoing involvement in the project, make sure you spell out his responsibilities and any contingencies for problems that might arise if he does not meet them.

For example, if you are writing, designing, and printing a brochure for the general manager of one of your operating divisions, it would be customary for him to approve the piece at various points along the way. You would probably let him read the draft of the manuscript and make changes if desired, suggest he review and approve the layout, and look at the printer's proof. His responsibility to look at and approve these items quickly should be a contingency of meeting the final deadline or coming in on budget. If you have to incur rush charges because approvals were delayed, responsibility should rest with the approver. Make sure in your proposal (in this example it would most likely be a standardized or memorandum proposal) that your reader understands his responsibilities and the consequences of not meeting them.

A clear definition of your reader's responsibilities will avoid misunderstandings or problems later.

MAPPING OUT A WORK PROGRAM

The first thing to be identified in the work program is what the end product, or *deliverable,* as the consultants call it, is going to be. If the finished product is going to be a prototype of a new product and engineering specifications for manufacturing it, specifically state that fact at the beginning of the work plan. If it is a project that will culminate in a report, describe the report and the elements that it will include.

After you have identified the end product, work backward and tell the reader how you are going to get there. Break each job down into separate tasks and identify each subtask or part. If appropriate, use a diagram or chart to detail each of the elements and illustrate the flow of work and how each task relates to the others.

Be sure to make allowances in your work program for testing

systems or machinery and for training people who will be required to perform unfamiliar duties as a result of this new project or activity. If publications or training manuals will be necessary, show when they will be produced and what will be included in them.

Also, include in your work plan arrangements for turning the project over to those who will maintain it, if appropriate. If, for example, your assignment is to install a system that others will operate and maintain, include a detailed plan for transferring responsibility for the system with no interruption in service or output. Affix a final date for turnover and detail the steps that must be accomplished (and when) before the turnover is made.

REPORTING REQUIREMENTS AND INTERVALS

Every decision maker likes to be reassured that he made the right decision. That's why, when you buy a new appliance, someone calls you up to make sure it is working properly and offers you an inexpensive service agreement. That's also why the manufacturer gives you a warranty. Each is a reassurance that, if the product breaks down, all the money you spent is not down the drain. The manufacturer will fix it for you so you can expect it to perform in the manner you thought it would when you bought it and for the length of time you were promised.

Do the same thing for your proposal decision makers. Give them a warranty that everything is going to work the way you promised. That warranty is in the form of regular reporting about the progress of the project. Include a schedule in your proposal that shows how often you will report and the form your reports will take. Will you provide monthly written summaries and a detailed report once each quarter at a meeting with the management group? If so, include each of these reporting times in your schedule.

Also, as mentioned earlier in the chapter, include checkpoints in the production schedule that require approval before proceeding any further. Include those checkpoints, the issue dates of written reports, and meeting dates for oral reports in your master schedule.

11

Proposals—The Finishing Touches

"I never did anything worth doing by accident; nor did any of my inventions come by accident."

Thomas Alva Edison

If the recipients of your proposal read it carefully and are impressed with the fact that the entire proposal exactly addressed their needs, this is no accident. It is, rather, the result of careful research to determine their needs and thoughtful writing to relate your service or your proposed project to their needs.

The features and benefits approach to writing, as it's called, not only describes the features of the service you are offering or the project or activity you are suggesting but relates those features to the recipients as benefits. It tells the readers what the service or activity will do for them.

The approach you use in writing to your audience will depend on your relationship with members of it and their knowledge of the topic at hand. If you are proposing a project that the recipients of the proposal know very little about, you will need to educate them and, at the same time, persuade them.

You cannot educate and persuade your readers by using "boilerplate" or verbiage that is general in nature and used again and again in similar proposals. Boilerplate may have a place in certain

143

general sections, but not in the portions of the proposal in which you are attempting to persuade your reader. Persuasion requires a careful relating of features and benefits to the real and perceived needs of your readers.

The features and benefits approach to writing is really nothing more than what we talk about through this book: looking at the situation from the reader's point of view. It cannot be overemphasized, especially in a proposal.

Let me give you an example. For the last few years I believed that there was a need for a book like this, one that would deal with the problems faced by writers of reports, interoffice proposals, letters, and memos. That belief was based largely on my experience in teaching writing seminars and the frequent requests I received to recommend good references in the field.

When I learned that a publishing company was planning to publish such a book and was looking for an author, I immediately telephoned to inquire about the project. An editor invited me to send a proposal.

As I saw the situation, I had two sales to make. The editor was already sold on the idea in general, but I had to persuade him that my approach was the best and that I was the one person who could do this book better than anyone else. And the idea had to be presented in such a fashion that he could sell my book to the other editors and the publisher.

Naturally, these people would be difficult to convince. They publish over one hundred books each year and reject thousands more. So I tried to make it easy for them. I emphasized the interest I had observed in various seminars in such a book, my experience in the field, and other unique attributes I could bring to the project. They didn't know me, so I had to establish credibility.

It worked. After a review of my proposal, writing samples, and some further discussion, we made a deal, and I began the book. The secret of success, I'm convinced, was looking at the proposal from the point of view of my audience.

PROPOSAL WRITING CHECKLIST

As you begin to finalize your proposal, review your approach to the project and all its elements to make certain that you are presenting your idea in the best possible way and that you have included all the information you should have.

Audience Analysis

- As you read the draft of your proposal, does it come through clearly that you have considered the needs of the decision makers and are presenting a proposal based on their point of view?
- Have you considered any secondary audiences? Are there others who may review copies of the proposal and have some influence in the final decision? If so, have you addressed their needs and interests?
- Does the proposal provide too much detail for your audience? Does it provide too little?
- Is your proposal too hard-sell for this audience? Is it hard-sell enough?
- What is the audience's reaction likely to be? Will it be positive, negative, or neutral?
- What is the audience's level of knowledge about the subject? Is your proposal too technical for the audience, or is it not technical enough?
- How receptive are your readers to new ideas?
- How does the audience usually respond to proposals like this one? Are they decisive, or do they postpone difficult decisions?

Transmittal Memo

- Did you include a transmittal memo? If not, why?
- Does your transmittal memo tell the reader why you are issuing the proposal?
- Does it call the reader's attention to key portions of the proposal that may be of special interest?
- Does it identify any contingencies or conditions governing terms of the proposal?
- Does your transmittal memo include an action step? Will the reader know what to do next?

Table of Contents

- Do you need a table of contents?
- Is your table of contents descriptive enough?
- Did you double-check the page references to make sure they are correct?
- Are all the titles on the contents page the same as in the proposal?
- Is it convenient for the reader to use?

List of Tables and Illustrations

- Do you need a list of tables and illustrations?
- Can it be combined with the table of contents?
- Are all the table and illustration headings correct, and do they appear exactly the same in the proposal?

Executive Summary

- Is your proposal long enough that you need to include an executive summary?
- How long should the summary be?
- Does your executive summary include all the key points?
- Do you emphasize the most important elements of the proposal in the summary?
- Is it interesting? Will it make the reader want to know more about the subject?
- Is it concise and to the point?
- Is it easy to read and understand?
- Is it persuasive?

Introduction

- Does the introduction serve as the focal point to get your reader started?
- Does it get your reader attuned to the way you were thinking when you wrote the proposal?
- Does it outline your approach to the project and why you selected this approach over others that you rejected?
- Does it identify any problems or limitations in the scope of the project or service?

- Do you identify key parts of the proposal?
- Did you include a call for action that reinforces the action step in your transmittal letter or memo?

Text or Body of the Proposal

- Did you include enough information? Did you include too much?
- Are sections of the proposal weighted according to their importance to each other and the entire proposal?
- Does it proceed smoothly from one idea or concept to the next, or do you need to add some transition sentences?
- Did you clearly state the objective of the proposal?
- Did you write the proposal to the point of view of the reader?
- Does it read as if it is all boilerplate?
- Is it too technical or not technical enough?
- Have you addressed the issue of technology?
  1. Have you reviewed the available technology and compared the advantages and disadvantages of various systems or pieces of equipment?
  2. Does your reader know that you are using technology that is state-of-the-art or what is most appropriate in this instance?
  3. Did you include flowcharts or other illustrations to show relationships among machines, computers, etc.?
  4. Have you made provisions for contingencies?

- Have you addressed the issue of people?
  1. Have you selected the right people for the job and conveyed their credentials to the decision makers reviewing the proposal?
  2. Should you include resumes of key members of the project team?
  3. Do you have a large enough staff? Is it too large?
  4. Did you include a detailed estimate of the amount of time and the number of people it will take?
  5. Did you include an organization chart?
  6. Did you include enough managers and supervisors in your staffing estimate?

7. Did you allow for vacations, sick leaves, and downtime?
8. Have you included examples of similar successful projects performed by members of your staff as individuals or as a group?
9. Did you include schedules detailing when various jobs will be completed and by whom?
10. Does your schedule include reporting relationships and the frequency and types of reports?

- Have you addressed the issue of service?
  1. Will ongoing service be required as part of this project?
  2. If so, have you assured your readers that adequate provisions have been made to ensure quality, timely service?
  3. Will you be using outside suppliers? What provisions have you made to ensure timely, quality service from them?
  4. At some point, will you be turning the project over to someone else who will be responsible for its continuing operations? If so, does your plan include provisions for ensuring an orderly transition?
  5. Is your service plan detailed enough? Too detailed?
  6. Have you provided enough information in a persuasive enough fashion for the reader to be convinced that the area of service is well provided for?

- Have you addressed the issue of budgets and costs?
  1. Are your estimates accurate?
  2. Are they believable?
  3. Did you provide enough or too little detail?
  4. Have you compared budgets and costs to other points of reference, such as previous year's figures or similar projects?
  5. Have you broken down the costs every way the reader might?
  6. Do all your figures balance and the columns foot?
  7. How does your budget request compare to others? Are you higher, lower, about the same? Does it matter?
  8. Have you identified any conditions or contingencies connected with cost estimates?
  9. Does your budget allow for start-up costs, service contracts, consulting fees, etc.?

10. Did you include travel expenses, handbooks and manuals, or other fees and expenses connected with training programs?
11. If a financial expert reads your budgets and cost estimates, will he be able to cast doubt on their accuracy? Can he relate them to other company financial statements?

Exhibits and Appendices

- Have you included an appendix? Should you?
- Is the right kind of information presented and in sufficient quantity?
- What is the length of the exhibits section compared to the rest of the proposal? Is it unduly long or short?
- Are exhibits clearly titled?
- If exhibits are referenced in the text of the proposal, are the page numbers correct?
- Are the exhibits and appendices listed in the table of contents?
- Is there information in the text of the proposal that belongs in an appendix?

Maintaining Your Objectivity

As you go through the proposal process, from the beginning of the strategy sessions, through the planning, writing, and production phases, you become very involved in the project and thus usually lose your objectivity. You may find yourself defending portions of the proposal in meetings simply because you wrote them and think they should be included.

When this happens, take a step back and rethink your reasons for including the information in the first place or for writing it the way you did. Others who have not been involved as intimately in the writing may have a better perspective. This is not to say that you shouldn't defend your ideas, but you should be open to suggestions for improvement without being offended.

To enhance objectivity further, it is a good idea at some point when the proposal is near completion to ask someone who has not been involved in the project at all to read it as though he were the recipient of the proposal charged with making final approval. Ask that person to test not only the logic and persuasiveness of the presentation but the mechanics and appearance as well. Make sure the reader can find sections of the report by checking the table of contents and scanning the headings and that the illustrations are helpful and in the proper locations.

And check one more time to make sure your close is strong enough and clear enough. If, after he has read the proposal, your reader doesn't know what to do and why, you have wasted your time and effort as well as that of your staff and others involved in the project.

RESUMES OF PROJECT STAFFERS

To enhance the credibility of the people staffing the project you may wish to include resumes detailing their background and experience and any special qualifications they may have that make them especially suited for this project.

If you do include resumes, don't treat them as a relatively unimportant appendix and let everyone write the resume according to personal preference. Be sure you read and edit every one with the same care you do the rest of the proposal. The resumes should be slanted specifically toward this project; otherwise, they are just useless boilerplate.

Most people who have been in business for any length of time have done many different jobs. The job of the proposal writer is to relate diverse career information to this particular project. General qualifications should be included only if they enhance this effort. Important civic and business affiliations are examples of general information that does not necessarily relate to a specific project but enhances the resume, because such examples humanize the individual and show that he is keeping current professionally, as well as contributing to the professional community.

Write the resumes in an active, positive style and emphasize accomplishments instead of responsibilities. Everyone has responsibilities. How well they perform those responsibilities is what is important to the reader. Examples of outstanding performance might include making or saving substantial amounts of money, installing new systems to improve the efficiency of the operation, and developing management techniques that improved productivity.

Be sure all resumes are consistent. Use a similar style and pay particular attention to the length of each. In contrast with resumes used in a job search, where you may want to include more information, a proposal resume should be limited to one page. Single-space the information in the resume and double-space between paragraphs.

The information contained in each resume should be in keeping with the individual's status in the organization. Managers should emphasize management experience, engineers should emphasize engineering achievements, and the like. In addition, within the various specialties weight the resumes according to the experience and achievements of the individuals. Don't, for example, have a page packed with relatively minor accomplishments for a junior staffer while the senior person on the project has a modest half-page summary of a long and distinguished career.

On page 152 is an example of a proposal resume written to emphasize the accomplishments instead of the responsibilities.

PROPOSAL COVERS

If you have taken the time and trouble to build a very good proposal, you should spend some time and money making a good package for it. The first impression your reader forms when he looks at the package will influence his opinion of the total product.

Some types of proposals lend themselves particularly well to interesting graphic treatments. If you are proposing the construction of a new facility, for example, an artist's rendering of the building would make a beautiful cover. A sample advertisement for a proposed advertising campaign would serve equally well.

If, however, none of these natural graphic elements are available, it is possible to design a visually pleasing cover using just type. For a little variety you may wish to print the cover in a solid color and reverse the words out of it. Your company's graphics or advertising department or your printer can show you how to do this.

You may wish to add a little extra to the cover by including your company's logo as a design element. If you do, check your corporate identification manual to make sure you are using the logo in an approved fashion. If you are uncertain about permissible use of your logo, check with your public relations department.

STEPHEN W. BROOKS

Mr. Brooks has been selected to handle facilities and capital equipment lease negotiations for the expansion of our manufacturing capability outlined in this proposal. He has extensive experience in this area with our firm and in previous positions with other companies prior to joining us in 1975. Some recent examples of related experience include having:

- placed $2.5 million in capital equipment leases with various sources in connection with the construction of our Newark, New Jersey, plant;
- planned and executed optimum lease arrangements as needed in diverse situations, including shirttail leases, lessor's lessor leases, and international lease transactions;
- negotiated more than $35 million in leases for the company's largest manufacturing joint venture;
- initiated an aggressive lease negotiation policy that resulted in substantial savings to the company.

Prior to joining our company Mr. Brooks was a leasing officer with a major U.S. bank, where he was responsible for supervising the leasing marketing team in a five-state region. Significant achievements during his five-year tenure with the company included having:

- improved group leasing sales by 125 percent in a period of three years;
- placed in the top five in lease placements for the bank for two consecutive years;
- opened new territories and established important new accounts, which previously had no relationship with the bank.

Other experience in finance and leasing includes experience with marketing leases through privately held lease brokers and work as portfolio manager for a real estate investment firm with holdings of more than $50 million.

PROPOSAL PACKAGING

How you package your final product will depend on what services are available to you and how much time you have. Many internal print shops have some bindery facilities and may be able to provide spiral or thermal binding (heat sealing at the spine). Many commercial printers offer similar services, in addition to saddle stitching (stapling it in the center like a magazine), perfect binding (gluing the pages at the spine and wrapping the cover around it), and other specialized forms of binding.

A wide variety of notebook binders is available from stationery and office supply stores, including some with a transparent sleeve on the front in which you can insert a printed piece designed especially for the proposal. Many notebooks offer an optional pocket in the back for inserting brochures or other loose material that may accompany the proposal.

If your proposal is relatively short, you may select protective acetate covers in a variety of colors that come with a slip-on spine to hold the pages in place. These are also available from your stationery or office supply store.

Whatever method you choose for packaging your proposal, make sure it reflects the work and thought that went into its production.

12

Reports—Preplanning for Best Results

"Thinking is the hardest work there is, which is the probable reason why so few engage in it."

Henry Ford

As with a proposal, thinking about the report beforehand and how it is likely to be perceived by the reader will in large measure determine whether the report accomplishes its mission. Clearly defining the mission of the report and looking at it from the audience's point of view are critical to its effectiveness.

Planning the writing of the report should be a continuous process throughout the information-gathering phase, should be refined during audience analysis, should be distilled to its essence in the outline, and should be purified for the reader in the final written document.

As writer of the report your role is different from that of information gatherer, scientist, researcher, or analyzer of data. All the information you have gathered, studied, and drawn conclusions from must now be conveyed to other interested parties, usually with the intention of stimulating some action.

Your report may be documentation of previous activities or transactions, distribution of information, an analysis of conditions, a recommendation for actions to be pursued, or a combination of several of these elements. You may have gathered information from several primary sources and reviewed pertinent secondary information; and the data may be sprinkled with your own conclusions and recommendations.

This collection of data, the results of research and experiments and opinions, must now be organized, analyzed, interpreted, and explained in a manner that can easily be understood and acted on by your readers. The report is the delivery of all the work that has gone on before. Your effectiveness in performing the research will be blunted if the report is poorly written or presented in a visual format that is difficult to follow.

PURPOSE OF THE REPORT

Reasons for generating reports are as many and as varied as the companies and employees that develop them. The report may be part of a regularly scheduled reporting system from your department that aids top management in making day-to-day decisions about how to run the business, or it may be a special report generated one time only to analyze a particular situation. Naturally, the purpose of the report will govern the point of view, the writing style, and the amount of information provided in the report. A regular monthly report may be an almost fill-in-the-blanks type, while a special analysis requires the full treatment.

Report Checklist

Before beginning the report, ask yourself the following questions to pinpoint the exact purpose of the report.

1. How much does my reader know about the subject?
2. How wide is the distribution of the report?
3. Are there any hidden audiences?
4. Is my reader expecting the report, or will it be a surprise?
5. What action, if any, do I want my reader to take?
6. What is the single most important idea that I want to convey to my reader?
7. How long must the report be to accomplish the purpose?
8. How detailed should it be?
9. How much supporting documentation will I need?
10. Should I provide other related documents as supplementary or background information?

11. Have others in the company generated similar reports that might be helpful in determining style, length, format, etc.?
12. Is this report really necessary?

Once you have determined the need for and the precise purpose of your report, writing it should be considerably easier.

GENERAL TYPES OF REPORTS

As with most written communications, to some degree all reports are informative, expressive, directive, or a combination of all these characteristics. You may first inform the reader about a situation, then express your conclusions based on your research, and finally offer recommendations or directives based on your findings.

Within that framework, there are several variations or types of reports, classified according to subject matter, organization, length, and frequency.

Standardized Reports

Some types of reports recur with such regularity that writers of the reports develop a standard form for presenting the information and may preprint forms with space provided for fill-in-the-blanks commentary.

Typical standardized reports include monthly or quarterly financial reports, weekly activity reports, sales reports, and conference reports (see example in Chapter 16).

Some companies may have standardized reports that follow a prescribed format and order of presentation to give executives a brief, easy-to-read analysis of the problem and a concise solution to the problem. Evolved from staff and technical reports, this report includes the following:

1. *Identifying information.* This introductory section includes the five *w*s of writing—who, what, where, when, and why. It identifies the sender and receiver of the report, the date, the subject of the report, and why it is being issued (regular monthly report, special study, etc.).
2. *The problem or objective of the report.* This section should

include a precise description of the problem or the objective of the study and a brief statement of the scope of the study or methods used to gather the information.

3. *Findings or discussion related to the problem.* This portion of the report deals with information gathered to determine the problem, analysis of data, and supporting information necessary to understand the nature and extent of the problem.
4. *Conclusions.* In this part of the report the facts, findings, and judgment and expertise of the writer are applied to the problem to arrive at the conclusions that relate to the problem and lead to the next portion of the report.
5. *Recommendations.* The type of report, its scope and objectives, as well as company policy, tradition, and authority of the writer will determine whether to include recommendations as part of the report. In most cases, however, the recommendation is the logical finish for a problem-solving report.

Letter or Memo Reports

Generally the least formal type of report, letter or memo report may be used when the subject matter is simple and the amount of information to be conveyed is brief.

Letters might be used to communicate information between persons from different divisions in the same company in slightly more formal situations or when there is a likelihood that copies may be sent to others outside the company. Memos, on the other hand, are usually informal and used strictly for interoffice communications.

Memo reports may begin with the identification of the writer, recipient, and subject matter and then continue by reporting the information without an introduction or other explanatory information. (See Chapter 16 for an example of a memo report.)

Short Reports

In order of formality, the short report falls somewhere between the memo or letter report and a formal report. It is more formal than a letter but not as formal as a comprehensive report. It is ideal for a problem that calls for a formal report but one that can be solved relatively easily and reported on briefly.

The length of a short report, like all reports, varies with the amount of material to be covered and the complexity of the information being presented. Usually, however, short reports consist of a title page and between one and ten pages of actual text.

The short report may begin with a summary and conclusion and include recommendations at the beginning, or it may begin with introductory remarks, present the subtitled information, and end with the summary, conclusion, and recommendations.

Committee Minutes and Reports

Depending on which expert you read or listen to, committee minutes and reports may or may not be considered formal reports. In the real business world, however, they are used frequently and as such require the same attention as other types of reports.

The increasing use of committees in modern management structures and traditionally in civic, business, and professional societies underscores the need for effective communication among various special subgroups of larger organizations.

If you are selected to keep the minutes of a meeting, the difficulty of the assignment will depend to some degree on the skill and preparation of the chairman. If a written agenda has been prepared for the meeting, and the meeting is conducted in an orderly fashion, keeping the minutes simply requires noting motions and other actions taken by the committee.

The order of presentation of the minutes may vary according to the group, but the most common arrangement is chronological. The minutes begin with a formal reporting of the time and place of the meeting and the members present. Then the progress of the meeting is reported chronologically, with numbered paragraphs dealing with each topic discussed.

Remember, the principal purpose of the minutes is to show for the record what went on at the meeting and to communicate the results to other interested groups. Don't make the minutes so complicated and boring that no one can or will read and understand what happened.

Technical Reports

Technical reports are similar to other types of extensive reports, with the principal difference being only the type of information presented in the report. Because of the complexity and, in some cases, specialization of the information presented, the technical report may devote more space to methodology used to arrive at certain information and may lead the reader through a series of experiments or logic to demonstrate how the problem was solved or the findings arrived at.

Otherwise the technical report is essentially the same in presentation as other types of long, formal reports. Often technical reports are issued from the same department or organization so frequently that the form and order of presentation are reasonably standard to avoid "reinventing the wheel" every time a report on a new topic is issued.

Internal Audit Reports

Another type of formal report with generally standard methods of presentation is the internal audit report. Traditional internal audit reports deal with financial information gathered by the company's internal auditors and reported to the directors and top management of the company. As business has grown more sophisticated, however, so have internal audit departments, which now frequently engage in other types of activity in addition to verification of financial data.

Auditors may be asked to conduct an operational audit to make sure the company's human and financial resources are used to best advantage, or they may be charged with verifying the company's physical and financial assets to make sure they are valued properly and managed correctly. And, of course, auditors are ever on the alert to discover fraud or theft in the course of examinations. All of these activities, despite their differences in character and scope, are reported in essentially the same style and format.

The Institute of Internal Auditors suggests that internal audit reports contain the following elements.

- Executive Summary Report;
- Foreword or Introduction;

- Purpose and Scope;
- Opinion (optional); and
- Findings and Recommendations.

The Institute emphasizes that increasing numbers of practitioners do include recommendations for correcting problems or situations rather than simply reporting existing conditions and leaving it to management to find ways to solve them.

Formal Reports

If your situation calls for a full-scale study and a final formal report upon its conclusion, preplanning is especially important. As indicated earlier in this chapter, the final written document is the result of all the work that has preceded it, and the report's success will depend on how well each of the steps was performed. Classify information according to the way you intend to use it as you gather and analyze it, and writing the report will be much easier.

Some elements of a report are optional, depending on its length, purpose, and use, while others are essential to convey your message in a fashion that is convenient for the reader. The decision as to what to include is yours; include what is necessary to accomplish your purpose.

Depending on your reasons for generating the report, you may wish to include any or all of the following:

- *Transmittal letter or memorandum.* If the report is to be issued to a small, select group of readers, a transmittal letter or memo may be used to prepare the reader for the report or tell him something about it. The type of information included in a transmittal letter or memo might be the purpose of the report, reasons for developing it, or the way in which the information should be used. The transmittal letter or memo is used simply to establish communication between the sender of the report and its recipient. It can convey any message the sender wishes.
- *Report cover.* Many organizations maintain a graphic arts staff to assist with enhancing the visual presentation of all documents produced by the company, and staff artists are

available to help design a cover for important reports. If the report is significant, both in size and in content, and no staff artist is available to assist, you may wish to engage a commercial (free-lance) artist to design a cover for you.

- *Flyleaf or title fly.* There is no reason other than pure tradition to include a title fly. The only information it contains is the report title, which most likely appears on the cover and the title page as well.

- *Title page.* This page includes the title of the report and other pertinent information about the report, such as its writer and recipient or the person and/or department that ordered the report.

- *Preface.* If the distribution of the report is too wide to warrant a personal letter or memo to recipients, or if the author of the report simply prefers to present the information in this fashion, the preface may be substituted for a transmittal letter or memo. The information contained might be essentially the same as that included in a transmittal document, or it might be a statement about the report that its author wishes to make before the reader begins the formal report.

- *Foreword.* The foreword, if it is used, is usually written by someone other than the author of the report. He may be the person who commissioned the report or have some other affiliation with the information being presented, or he may be lending his support to the cause. Whatever his interest in the report, the writer of the foreword should be identified and his affiliation clarified.

- *Table of contents.* If you are issuing a long (more than ten pages) report, use a table of contents to help your reader identify key portions of the report and their location in the report.

- *List of tables and illustrations.* To provide a ready reference for your reader, you may wish to include a guide to the illustrations used in the report. Neither the table of contents nor the list of illustrations should be prepared until the report is finished, to make sure that both are all-inclusive and that the pagination is correct. As with proposals, if you only have a few illustrations, you may decide to include them on the contents page.

- *Acknowledgments.* Although acknowledgments are more typically used in books, you may wish to recognize those who made an important contribution to the report or thank those who were particularly helpful in gathering the information for the report. This section is not to be confused with the bibliography or reading lists, which acknowledge and reference other published works.

- *Abstract.* An abstract is the condensation of the report in the order of presentation and weighted according to the amount of information about each topic that is included in the final report. Sometimes called a *précis,* the abstract may be written based on the table of contents or by selecting topic sentences from key paragraphs in the report. It is difficult for an author to capsulize all his work and research into an abstract, and this may be accomplished more effectively by asking an independent third party to abstract the report. In interoffice communication, abstracts of reports might be sent to potential recipients to determine their level of interest; however, abstracts are more typically used by outsiders such as editors and publishers who are considering publication of your work or by professional societies reviewing abstracts to schedule technical papers for presentation at conferences, workshops, and seminars and to certify them for continuing education credits.

- *Executive summaries.* As the name implies, the executive summary is designed to provide executives and other decision makers with a condensed version of the report with emphasis placed on the elements the author believes to be most important in the decision-making process. It differs from an abstract in that it does not necessarily provide a detailed summary of the report in order of presentation but, rather, provides *selective* information the author deems important, arranged according to the most effective method of presentation. Executive summaries may be bound into the report or may be separate documents. If your audience includes executives who are interested in a synopsis of the problem and others who are detail oriented, you can meet the needs of both by providing an executive summary that highlights pertinent information, accompanied by the full report for those who require more detail.

- *Introduction to the report.* In the introduction the author brings all the readers to the same point of departure before beginning the main body or text of the report. For example, you may wish to review the reasons for the report, the scope and limitations, and your methods for collecting the data that you will present in the report.
- *Report body or text.* This is the portion of the report in which the information is presented, the problems identified, the solutions suggested, and the battles won and lost. All the other elements are embellishments. The payoff in advance planning is especially apparent in the report text. If, at the outset of the investigation or analysis, you determined the audience objectives or mission of the report, as well as the scope and limitations, established deadlines, and had a good idea of how the report should be organized—then worked your plan—chances are good that your report will be informative, timely, persuasive, and effective. Conversely, if you generated the report as an afterthought, it will most likely be apparent to your readers.
- *Summary and conclusions.* How you end your report is optional, but formal reports usually end with a summary of the data presented or the analysis performed, the conclusions that were drawn as a result, and, if appropriate, recommendations for solving the problem. You may elect to end the report by suggesting other actions that should be taken in the future, such as a specialized study on a topic that was not explored fully in this report.
- *Appendices.* To make the report as readable as possible, supporting information such as other studies, detailed results of experiments, sample questionnaires, transcripts of interviews, work papers, and the like are included in the appendix section. Each exhibit in the appendix should be labeled clearly for easy identification and may be referenced in the text by something like: "See Exhibit I—Statistical Comparison of Rainfall in the United States."
- *Bibliography.* If your report requires extensive secondary research (published information), you should include a bibliography that lists the sources of that information. How the information should be listed and the treatment of footnotes is covered in Chapter 15.

13

Reports—Organizational Methods

"In the modern world of business, it is useless to be a creative, original thinker unless you can also sell what you create. Management cannot be expected to recognize a good idea unless it is presented to them by a good salesman."

David Mackenzie Ogilvy

Determining the method of organizing the report, like all other aspects of producing it, depends in part on the final objective—what you are selling. You may be selling an idea or approach to solving a problem or persuading others to accept your line of reasoning—all variations of selling, but selling, nevertheless.

Orators long ago developed two approaches to conveying their ideas and bringing audiences around to their way of thinking. The first method, *deductive reasoning,* begins with a theory or premise from which applications or conclusions are deduced. Conversely, the *inductive method of reasoning* presents the facts or arguments and leads to a conclusion based on the information presented.

In report writing the same two broad classifications are used, though there may be many variations on these two general themes.

DEDUCTIVE METHOD

The deductive method of presentation in report writing (sometimes called the *direct method*) begins by stating the conclusion and recommendations, then presents the supporting documentation. This method of presentation is especially useful in shorter reports and those that do not require great amounts of detail to lead the reader to the conclusion.

An example of the deductive method might take the following form in a memo report.

To: C. P. Jones   September 23, 19xx

From: A. B. Brennen
           Vice President, Human Resources

Subject: Flexible Hours

After careful consideration, the Human Resources Department has reached the conclusion that we should offer our employees flexible working hours. This conclusion is based on the following.

1. Because of our isolated location, we do not have a large population base from which to recruit employees.

2. Our salaries for clerical workers are below average, and our present financial position will not allow us to raise them in the foreseeable future.

3. Many of our employees are working mothers and would like the option of arranging their work schedules around responsibilities at home.

4. Staggered arrival and departure times would relieve congestion at the plant entrance.

5. Having some employees in the office early in the morning and later in the afternoon would allow us to extend our order processing in the Eastern and Pacific time zones.

6. Flexible hours would allow us to offer an inducement to current employees to stay with the company and give us a recruiting advantage other than salaries--one that could be offered at no expense to the company.

If you agree that this is a desirable course of action, let's put it on the agenda for the next department head meeting and discuss optimum methods of implementation.

INDUCTIVE METHOD

In the inductive (or *indirect*) method of presentation the report would begin with a statement of the problem or subject of the report, then present information or data collected, move on to any analysis necessary, and end with the conclusions and recommendations.

The same memo report, using the inductive method of presentation, would be as follows.

To: C. P. Jones   September 23, 19xx
            President

From: A. B. Brennan
            Vice President, Human Resources

Subject: Flexible Hours

The Human Resources Department has conducted
a study to determine if there are additional
incentives we can offer to present and prospective
employees. After interviewing several clerical
workers, and reviewing appropriate census data,
we determined the following.

1. Because of our isolated location, we do
    not have a large population base from which
    to recruit employees.

2. Our salaries for clerical workers are
    below average, and our financial position
    will not allow us to raise them in the
    foreseeable future.

3. Many of our employees are working mothers
    and would like the option of arranging
    their work schedules around responsibilities
    at home.

4. Staggered arrival and departure times
    would relieve congestion at the plant entrance.

5. Having some employees in the office
    early in the morning and later in the
    evening would allow us to extend our
    order processing in the Eastern and
    Pacific time zones.

6. Flexible hours would allow us to offer an
    inducement to current employees to stay
    with the company and would give us a
    recruiting advantage other than salaries--
    one that could be offered at no expense

    to the company.

It is our recommendation, based on these
findings, that we offer flexible hours to our
employees. If you agree that this is a desirable
course of action, let's put it on the agenda for
the next department head meeting and discuss
optimum methods of implementation.

Generally, the deductive type of presentation works best for shorter, less complicated reports, and the inductive method is best suited for complex, lengthy reports. As with any generalization, however, there are exceptions. You are the best judge of your situation and of the most effective method of presenting your findings.

Once you have decided whether to use the inductive or deductive method of reporting you can decide other organizational patterns that will determine how and in what order the material will be included in the report. At this point in the development of the report the goal is to further separate the material into classifications according to logical divisions that aid in understanding.

There are many complicated explanations and descriptions of report divisions developed by report writers, writing instructors, and authors of how-to books, but all are variations of the old five *w*s of journalism (who, what, where, when, and why) with, perhaps, the addition of how (making recommendations). Almost all reports are organized along the lines of one or more of these methods.

ORGANIZATION ACCORDING TO PERSONNEL OR DEPARTMENT (WHO)

To report on the material you have gathered by whom it affects, by department, or by the personnel involved in the situation is one alternative for presenting information in the report.

This method might also be used in a report describing the situation according to responsibilities of individuals involved or some attribute they share.

Some types of reports would quite naturally divide themselves into subsections by personnel. Examples might be reports on executive compensation levels, performance evaluations, bonuses, or reorganization of departments or other company entities. An outline for a report organized along "who" lines might be as follows:

```
             Executive Compensation Study

    I.  Introduction

        A.  Reasons for the study

        B.  Methodology used in the study

        C.  Scope of the study

   II.  Present Compensation

        A.  President

        B.  Vice-Presidents

            1.  Finance

            2.  Operations
```

        3. Marketing

        4. Public relations

        5. Research and development

        6. Human resources

    C. Corporate secretary and legal counsel

    D. Treasurer

III. Comparisons

    A. Industry

    B. Geography

IV. Summary and Conclusions

V. Recommendations

ORGANIZATION ACCORDING TO FUNCTIONS OR SPECIAL CHARACTERISTICS (WHAT)

The factors that are affected by or studied in a report are as many and as varied as the company and its products, its methods of marketing and manufacturing, or any other characteristic of the business. Some examples are organization according to quantity, function, event, element, characteristic, relationship, comparison, or order of importance in ascending or descending order.

An outline organizing information by what is involved might look like this:

Agency Occupancy Cost Analysis

I. Introduction

    A. Purpose of the study

    B. Methodology used

    C. Scope of the study

II.   Elements of Occupancy Cost

    A.   Rent

    B.   Utilities

    C.   Telephone service

    D.   Interior design

        1.   Furniture

        2.   Artwork and plants

    E.   Overhead

        1.   Corporate officers

        2.   Support staff

        3.   Printing and duplicating

III.   Alternative Methods of Allocation

    A.   Square footage

    B.   Number of personnel

    C.   Line of business

    D.   Number of clients

IV.   Summary and Conclusions

V.   Recommendations

In this example the analysis is conducted to determine the cost of occupying a building to apportion those costs to the various groups responsible for account management and sales according to some logical formula. The common characteristic of the study is cost per unit, whatever the unit happens to be.

This and the previous example both indicate that seldom, if ever, is one division of information entirely appropriate. Rather, combinations are usually used. In the first example the "who" was combined with a "what"—statistical comparisons—to provide a criterion for drawing conclusions. In the second example, to determine the most logical methods for allocating occupancy cost, the report writer must again use comparisons to demonstrate various approaches to assigning unit costs according to some other division of information, such as square footage, personnel, lines of business, or number of clients.

ORGANIZATION ACCORDING TO GEOGRAPHY (WHERE)

The "where" of reporting clearly is defined more easily, since it is done exclusively according to geography or location. Types of reports that could most effectively use geographic breakdowns of information are site selection studies, comparisons of sale by region, marketing studies by location, and the like.

A typical outline for a report organized according to geography might be done as follows.

MARKET PENETRATION

BY REGION

I.   Introduction

    A.   Purpose and scope of the study

    B.   Methodology and techniques used

II.   Present Market Penetration

    A.   Northwest

    B.   West

    C.   South

    D.   Southeast

    E.   Midwest

    F.   Southwest

III.   Projected Market Penetration by Region

    A.   Critical Assumptions

        1.   Economic influence

    2. Degree of industry maturation

    3. Competitive environment

  B. Controllable variables

    1. Management's growth expectations

    2. Research and experimentation (technological) influence

    3. Marketing support required.

IV. Summary and Conclusions

V. Recommendations

In this example, to provide a geographic comparison between present and projected market penetration, factors in section III that vary by region should be addressed individually by region. Economic influences, for example, differ from region to region and would affect market penetration differently in high-growth areas such as the so-called "Sun Belt" than in aging midwestern industrial centers.

ORGANIZATION ACCORDING TO TIME (WHEN)

If the material in the report lends itself to reporting according to time considerations, you may prefer this method of organization. Chronological reports or reports in which time is a principal consideration are examples. What happened and when are details often included in security reports and investigations, data from experiments, or reports on violations of company policy that may later need documentation for disciplinary actions. Other examples would include any report that might be used in legal proceedings in which precision is of utmost importance.

Salesmen's call reports might be organized chronologically to show the activity on an account as in the following example.

ACCOUNT REPORT:

AJAX TOOL AND DIE

I. Account Assignment

  A. April 1978 to May 1982--House Account

    B.   June 1983--Assigned to Pacific Northwest Region

  II. Activity

    A. House Account

      1. 1978 sales volume $50,000

      2. 1979 sales volume $183,000

      3. 1980 sales volume $175,000

      4. 1981 sales volume $190,000

      5. 1982 sales volume $120,000

      6. First half of 1983 sales volume $50,000

    B. Northwest Region

      1. First call July 7, 1982

      2. July 15, 1983; product test

      3. July 20, 1983; order placed for $300,000

      4. August 1 service call

      5. October 20 order placed for $160,000

 III. 1984 Account Sales and Service Plan

  IV. Summary and Conclusion

   V. Recommendations

ORGANIZATION ACCORDING TO CAUSE (WHY)

If the cause of some action is the most important element of your report, you may choose to organize your material around the reasons for the occurrence. An investigation into why a division or product line is losing money and an analysis to determine why a manufacturing facility is operating at below-average efficiency are some examples of topics that might be organized effectively along causal lines.

As a practical matter, the cause of problems would probably be included as a part of the total report, such as in audit reports that report not only the cause but the condition that exists as a result, the criterion or standard it should be measured against, and the effect of something happening that should not have.

An outline of a report emphasizing the cause of problems might be as follows.

PRODUCTIVITY ANALYSIS:

MONTEREY FACILITY

I. Introduction

    A. Purpose of the study

    B. Scope of the study

II. Findings

    A. Significant decline in productivity

    B. Criterion

        1. Industry standards

        2. Other company facilities

III. Causes of Productivity Decline

    A. Unrealistic management expectations

    B. Poor attitudes

    C. Improper maintenance of equipment

    D. Inefficient manufacturing work flow

    E. Insufficient quality control of raw materials

    F. Disorganized order entry and scheduling

IV. Summary and Conclusions

V. Recommendations

COMBINATIONS AND COMPARISONS

Because one element of a report is seldom enough to build an entire report on, most require at least one other element, if the document is to be meaningful. The condition of productivity decline in the preceding example, for instance, should be coupled with the causes for the decline, and comparisons should be provided against some known and accepted standard to give the reader a point of reference.

The purpose of the different organizational patterns is to provide a variety from which to select the one that best presents the information in each individual case. Select the method of presentation and the organizational pattern that best help your reader understand the report and all its subtleties.

Comparing one or more elements in the report aids in that understanding and has the added benefits of presenting the author as an objective writer and giving the reader a balanced view of the situation.

It is possible to organize the report around comparisons by subheading one item and then the item to which it is to be compared. Financial reports, for example, often compare current results to previous years to give the reader a ready reference for the company's performance. Results of an analysis, which examine each of the components of the financial reports and why the company performed as it did, may then be reported.

RECOMMENDATIONS (HOW)

Unless the purpose of your study is exclusively informational, your report should end with a recommendation for solving the problem, improving performance, or otherwise bringing about positive change from the results reported in the study.

Because of your familiarity with the material, you may assume that the reader knows more about the topic than he actually does and that the recommendations are implicit in the findings. Naturally you should not insult your reader's intelligence, but at the same time you should not leave him guessing either.

The best way to avoid either eventuality is to present your recommendations in a straightforward, tactful fashion. More complicated, more important, or longer recommendations might be included early in the section with shorter recommendations of lesser importance listed near the end of the section.

You should have decided during the planning stages exactly what you planned to accomplish. Keep that goal in mind as you present your recommendations. Organize the recommendation section to accomplish it. If you found an inordinate number of problems in your study, you may elect to omit some of the more insignificant ones to help the reader focus on the larger issues. As writer of the report, you must decide.

The recommendation section of the report is where the sale is made or lost. The organizational pattern and method of presentation should be aimed at making absolutely certain that you have done everything possible to have your recommendations adopted.

14

Writing the Report

"Writers seldom write the things they think. They simply write the things they think other folks think they think."

Elbert Green Hubbard

An important consideration in the production of any report is establishing credibility with a reader. As we read, most of us have a tendency to be a bit skeptical, particularly if the writer is trying to persuade us to do something or to think a certain way. We take a "show me" attitude and must be convinced.

The best way to establish credibility with your reader is to do your homework. Your knowledge of the subject and the careful research you have performed should immediately be apparent to your reader. If they are not, you have a credibility problem.

Some radio spots being run around the country advertising Dale Carnegie courses tell the story of an old craftsman who is working on a brass door. When a visitor asks, "How do you know when it's finished?" the old craftsman replies, "Sir, it's never finished; I just keep working on it until they come and take it away."

So it is with writing a report. To do the job perfectly it is possible to research and rewrite it forever. As a practical matter, at some point you must decide that you have accumulated enough information and get down to the business of writing the report. How do you know when you have reached that point? This is determined by a combination of three factors:

1. the amount of information available about the subject, including both primary and secondary information;
2. the audience's familiarity with the subject;
3. your level of comfort with the information you have assembled.

If any of these considerations has not been addressed, you are not yet ready to write. Surveying the literature available about a topic, reviewing trade articles, and analyzing your audience are accomplished relatively easily. Measuring your comfort level with the information, however, is more subjective and may not be so easy to do.

Performing the first two steps helps you get on the track toward developing an understanding of what is to be said, but the best single step toward becoming comfortable with your findings and recommendations is to be sure *you* understand the problem clearly and, then, to state it so the reader understands it equally well.

As you conducted interviews or reviewed published information about the topic of your report, you probably formed several conclusions along the way as new information was learned. You may have even been surprised by some of the findings and changed your views about some parts of the subject, but your reader hasn't had the advantage of reviewing all the information. He is depending on you to show him the way.

By clearly defining the problem and referring back to it as you write the report, you remind yourself that all the information you present in the report should relate to the problem or topic of the report. In fact, before beginning the actual writing of the report you may want to ask the people who commissioned the report to review the statement of the problem to make sure you are going in the right direction.

As you consider the problem mentally, it may take several forms. You may ask a question, for example, such as "Why are manufacturing costs so high?" or "What is our image in the marketplace?" Or you may state the problem in a declarative sentence. When you commit the problem to writing in the report, however, it should be stated formally. Write it clearly and succinctly so all readers of the report will know exactly what you set out to solve when you began the project.

SECTIONS OF THE REPORT

A review of the types of reports and a listing of possible elements of a report appear in Chapter 12. For use in this example, let's assume that this is a formal report. We have reviewed the list of possible elements and decided the following items best suit our needs for this report.

Cover
Title page
Preface
Table of contents
List of tables and illustrations
Executive summary
Introduction
Body or text
Summary and conclusion

We are to develop a consumer image study in our geographic area to identify traits of our customers and potential customers for the top management of our bank, Dominant Trust, to use in formulating a marketing strategy. Our results are to be presented in a formal report.

The scope of the report has been agreed on in advance.

Because of the complex nature of the material, we have selected the inductive or indirect method of presentation. That is, we will present the findings, then reach conclusions and make recommendations based on those findings. The method of organization will be determined by the findings.

OUTLINING THE REPORT

With the data assembled and analyzed, a list made of the elements to be included, and an organizational method and pattern selected, we are now ready to outline the report. The outline will be the guide for writing the report and will help determine the length and areas of emphasis. Any weaknesses in data or information gathered will show up at this point as well. If there is insufficient information to outline properly, further research may be necessary.

As in all writing and organization, the construction of the

outline should be parallel in presentation as well as in format. Do not mix complete sentences with phrases. If you select the topic outline format, use it throughout.

After you have listed the elements to be included in the report, outline the appropriate sections. Begin with the introduction and list the elements you plan to cover in it; then move on to the report body and text. After you have outlined the text, outline your summary and conclusions. If you already have a firm fix on your summary and conclusions, you may want to outline them first and then build the rest of the report around them, making sure everything else you present supports your conclusions. Very often, however, as you review the findings and organize them in order of presentation, you may identify key points for the summary and conclusion section. It is usually best to outline the report text first.

Other elements, such as the preface, table of contents, list of tables and illustrations, acknowledgments, and executive summary, should be written last to make sure you have all the pages, illustrations, lists, exhibits, etc., in order and that you have the perspective of the whole report before beginning to extract key portions of it.

In some cases you may prefer to outline the introduction after you have completed the report text outline, but in this instance the introduction will be fairly straightforward, and the elements to be included are already known.

Most marketing research studies, and many other types of reports as well, include a statement about the scope of the study, its objectives, and the methodology used to conduct the study. Therefore, we can comfortably outline the introduction at the beginning.

The subsections of the report will be organized around the findings, which, again, are already firmly fixed because the scope and objectives of the report established what we would research before the study was begun. Such preplanning simplifies the report writing portion of the project.

In this example the tables, illustrations, charts, and graphs—if any are to be included—would probably be determined in the actual writing process as opposed to during the outline stage. We know in the beginning that we will probably include tables that illustrate various findings and summaries of answers to various questions, but we may decide to include a chart or graph if the material is so complex that it is difficult to explain without an illustration. Exhibits and appendices are generally arrived at in the same way. If, during the narrative, we refer to a crosstabulation computer printout, for example, we may elect to include an example in the appendix or exhibit section.

This, then, is the outline of our report:

DOMINANT TRUST COMPANY

CONSUMER IMAGE STUDY

I. Introduction

    A. Scope of the study

        1. Geographic limits--Oak Forest and Forest Village Counties

        2. Subjects--heads of households responsible or coresponsible for the household's banking in households with either a bank or a savings and loan association

    B. Objectives of the study

        1. Determine bank awareness levels

        2. Develop image profile of ideal bank

        3. Where awareness exists, determine image profiles of our bank and principal competitors

        4. Profile users of such services as checkings, savings, and NOW accounts

        5. Ascertain demographic profile of our market's age, income, dual household

income, education, occupation,
marital status, household size, and
duration of residence

C. Methodology

   1. Develop survey questionnaire to meet
study objectives

   2. Interview 300 noncustomers and 100
customers

      a. Total of 200 male and 200 female
interviews

      b. One-half in Oak Forest County and
one-half in Forest Village County

   3. Statistical tests

      a. Chi-square

      b. T-test

      c. Analysis of variance and multiple
regression

II. Report Body or Text

A. Financial institution awareness in market
area

   1. Unaided awareness

2. 2. Aided awareness

   3. Total awareness

B. Service usage and market shares

   1. Incidence of service usage

   2. NOW accounts

       3. Checking accounts

       4. Certificates of deposits

       5. Savings account

       6. Money market funds

C. Behavioral characteristics

       1. Banks close to home

       2. Banks close to work

       3. Switching behavior

D. Demographic profile characteristics

       1. Duration of current residence

       2. Duration of Metroland residence

       3. Dwelling ownership

       4. Married with dual income

       5. Marital status

       6. Education

       7. Household size

       8. Age

       9. Annual household income

E. Bank image profiles in the Metroland market

       1. Multiple regression, image profile, and gap analysis

       2. Image attributes

          a. Basic attributes

          b. Primary attributes

          c. Double primary attributes

       3. Gap analysis

F. Conclusions and recommendations

1. Leader in the area; position the bank against all others

2. Market is large and homogeneous; little need to develop specialized target market programs because of perceived dominance

3. Perceived as friendly and low cost; continue to reinforce that image

4. Perceived as not as helpful as its competitors; marketing strategy should address this problem

5. Competitor Evermore National believed to be a better place to get a loan; strategy should address this issue

6. Two other competitors hold strong positions as offering fast service; position bank as a provider of fast service

7. Significant gap between Dominant Trust's image and that of the ideal bank in "Makes few errors in customer account" category; specific policy should be developed for handling errors and improving this image

WRITING THE REPORT

With the outline completed and the sections of the report identified, we are now ready to write the report. The following is an actual report prepared for a midwestern bank. Only the names, according to its author, Richard Fowler, president of Market Focus, a marketing research firm based in Chicago, "have been changed to protect the profitable."

The report was abbreviated substantially for inclusion in this book, and several tables and charts, as well as the appendix, were omitted because of space considerations. Nonetheless, what follows is still rather lengthy. However, to abbreviate it further would require the elimination of key portions which are essential to the report, resulting in a disservice to the reader.

MEMORANDUM

To: John Q. Jones   May 30, 19xx

From: Richard C. Fowler   Enclosures:
                                    Report
Subject: Consumer Image Study

Thank you for the opportunity to work with you
on this most important project. Both my staff and
I enjoyed it thoroughly and believe we have made a
significant contribution to the success of Dominant
Trust Company's future marketing efforts.

Your copy of the final report is attached. It
was circulated in draft form to key bank officers,
and their comments have been incorporated into the
report.

I call your attention to the executive summary
in the front of the report. There you will find
key elements of our findings summarized for convenient review.

We have included the detailed findings that
we believe you will find most useful and summarized
the data in tables and charts for easy reference.

For the most part the study reinforced our
belief that Dominant Trust is the market leader in
the areas in which we have chosen to operate, but
the study points up areas where the competition may
be gaining, as well as gaps in consumer perception
of Dominant's services versus their perception
of such services from an "ideal bank." Our
recommendations for dealing with those issues are
included as a part of the report.

I would suggest that the next step, if you
agree with our recommendations, would be to schedule
a meeting among senior bank officers, the marketing
department, and the advertising agency to develop
an implementation strategy. I will give you a call
in two weeks to discuss your reaction to the report
and our recommendations.

If, after reviewing the report, you have any
questions or you would like additional information
about any of the material covered, please let me
know.

Dominant Trust Company

Consumer Image Study

Prepared by:

Richard C. Fowler

DOMINANT TRUST COMPANY

CONSUMER IMAGE STUDY

Prepared by:

Richard C. Fowler

CONTENTS

PREFACE

At the outset of this project most of those involved agreed that Dominant Trust Company was the market leader. The degree of leadership, however, was subject to some speculation, as was consumer perception of the services offered.

We developed a questionnaire that addressed those key issues, and we interviewed a significant number of people to find precise answers to our questions. Some of those we interviewed were already customers of the bank; others were not.

Our findings reinforced our belief that Dominant Trust is the undisputed market leader, but also pointed up some areas for improvement.

One element of the study was a comparison of Dominant's services and those of competitors to a so-called "ideal bank." While none of us met the consumers' expectation of an ideal bank, Dominant Trust scored relatively good marks. Our recommendations for dealing with problem areas, capitalizing on strengths, and minimizing weaknesses are included in digest form in the executive summary and in their entirety in the conclusions and recommendations section of the main text of the report.

It is my firm conviction that the results of this study, properly applied, will make a significant contribution to the success of future marketing efforts.

Richard C. Fowler

LIST OF TABLES AND FIGURES

INTRODUCTION

The scope of this study was limited to the geographical limits of the counties of Oak Forest and Forest Village, which is the principal market area of Dominant Trust. Subjects of the study were heads of households either responsible or coresponsible for the household's banking in households with either a bank or a savings and loan deposit account.

Objectives

There were five specific objectives of the study:

- to determine bank awareness levels;
- to develop an image profile of an ideal bank;
- to determine, where awareness exists, the image profile of Dominant Trust Company and its two principal competitors, Maturing Bank and Evermore National;
- to profile users of such services as checking, savings, and NOW accounts; and
- to ascertain the demographic profile of our market with emphasis on age, income, dual household income, education, occupation, marital status, household size, and duration of residence.

Methodology

Using a questionnaire developed specifically to meet study objectives, telephone interviews were conducted at random during the month of April from a list of telephone numbers covering the Metroland market. The goal was 300 noncustomer interviews while maintaining a 50/50 quota of male/female subjects and a 50/50 quota of Oak Forest County/ Forest Village County residents.

The results were:

Noncustomers	300
Dominant Trust customers	106
Total	406
Male	48.5%
Female	51.5%
Oak Forest County	50.5%
Forest Village County	49.5%

Next, an additional 94 telephone interviews were conducted at random from a list of customer telephone numbers supplied by Dominant Trust. The same sex and county quotas were used. Combining the random market list interviews and the customer list interviews resulted in:

Noncustomers	305
Dominant Trust customers	195
Total	500
Male	50.1%
Female	49.9%
Oak Forest County	49.9%
Forest Village County	50.1%

The questionnaires were computer processed using a crosstabulation plan designed to provide information in the most desirable formats and comparisons.

Statistical tests used to analyze the results were chi-square, T-test, analysis of variance, and multiple regression. In all cases the criterion for statistical significance was p=.05, meaning that only in five times out of 100 or less would the observed difference be expected to have occurred purely on the basis of chance.

EXECUTIVE SUMMARY

Telephone surveys were conducted among heads of households either responsible or coresponsible for the banking in households with a bank or S&L deposit account. Quotas of 50/50 for male/female and Oak Forest County/Forest Village County were maintained.

First, 406 interviews were conducted from a random market list and used for awareness, service usage, market share, and image profile analyses. Second, an additional 94 interviews were conducted at random from a list supplied by Dominant Trust to make possible customer versus noncustomer comparisons of demographic profiles. The findings, conclusions, and recommendations are summarized below.

Findings

- On financial institution awareness Dominant

Trust was the clear leader in first
mentions (22.7 percent), unaided awareness
(44.6 percent), and total awareness (95.1
percent). On unaided awareness Maturing
Bank and Trust was second (28.8 percent),
and Evermore National was a close third
(24.4 percent).

- Likewise, Dominant Trust was the clear leader
  in main bank share (20.9 percent) and overall
  market share (26.1 percent). Maturing Bank
  and Trust was second in main bank share
  (12.6 percent) and in overall market share
  (16.5 percent). Evermore National was third
  in main bank share (7.1 percent) and in
  overall share (9.9 percent).

- Crosstabulation analysis revealed statistically
  significant differences in the demographic
  profiles for the incidence of service usage.

- Dominant Trust was also the leader in market
  share for NOW accounts (12.0 percent),
  checking (25.3 percent), Certificates of
  Deposit (CD) (15.0 percent), and savings
  (18.1 percent).

- About one-half of the respondents reported
  that the branch of their main bank used most
  often was closer to home, one-fourth said

7

it was closer to work, and one-fourth said
they used both about equally. Crosstabulation
analysis revealed statistically significant
differences for the demographic profiles of
those who orient to home and those who
orient to work.

● Switching main banks in the last twelve
months for reasons other than moving or
changing jobs was reported by 14 percent of
the respondents.

The demographic profile of Dominant Trust
customers was:

1. Median current residence of 8.5 years and
    average of 11.5 years.

2. Median Metroland residence of 22.0 years
    and average of 21.9 years.

3. Seven in ten owners and three in ten renters.

4. Among married people, almost two-thirds
    with dual incomes.

5. Also two-thirds married and one-third not
    married.

6. Three-fourths having some college or more,
    with about one-fourth having some graduate
    school or more.

7. Median household size of 3.2 and average
    of 3.0.

8

8. Median age of 42.6 years and average of
43.8 years.

9. Average annual household income of $33,000.

In comparison with competitors, Dominant Trust
attracted as customers people who:

- have lived at their current address longer,
  with an average duration of 11.5 years
  versus 9.8 years;

- have lived in the Metroland area longer, with
  an average duration of 21.9 years versus
  17.6 years.

- are less likely to be married (64.1 percent
  versus 73.1 percent and more likely to be
  single, divorced, separated, or widowed
  (35.4 percent versus 24.9 percent).

Analysis of the image attributes did not reveal
any submarkets with different image profiles
requiring target market programs. Analysis of the
image attributes most highly correlated with the
overall rating of a bank revealed two primary
attributes:

- "Friendly personnel" for Dominant Trust.

- "Helpful personnel" for Evermore National
  and Maturing Bank and Trust.

These two primary attributes were highly

correlated with each other and were not statistically different from one another in importance in rating the ideal bank.

On basic image attributes, those attributes where good performance is merely expected and poor performance can be disastrous, Dominant Trust did not perform poorly versus competitors.

All three banks ranked low in comparison to the ideal bank on the basic attribute "makes few errors in customer accounts."

The second most important attribute in Dominant Trust's image was "low service charges," while second position for Evermore National was "a good place to get a loan" and for Maturing Bank and Trust was "fast service." "Fast service" was also Evermore National's third most important attribute.

Recommendations

According to the results of the study, Dominant Trust should pursue the following activities in its marketing strategy.

- Continue communication with the market-place to assure dominance in bank awareness.
- Communicate with the market as a whole, rather than target special submarkets.

- Position Dominant Trust in advertising copy as the friendly, low-service-charge bank.
- Augment that position by emphasizing primary attributes of competitors, including:
  1. helpful personnel;
  2. a good place to get a loan; and
  3. fast service.
- Take advantage of the image gap in "makes few errors in customer accounts" by controlling the error rate and, more importantly, the handling of customers when an error occurs.
- Use demographic profiles on image attributes to guide media selection when attempting to improve an attribute rating.
- Without alienating current customers, expand the customer base by seeking people who are new to the area.
- Use differences in demographic profiles of those whose banking is oriented to home or oriented to work as a guide for branch level marketing.

- Use differences in demographic profiles
  on the incidence of service usage as a
  guide to marketing current services or
  developing new services to compete with
  money market funds.

DETAILED FINDINGS

Financial Institution Awareness
in the Metroland Market

All respondents were asked, "When you think
about financial institutions in the area, what is
the first one that comes to mind?" The results
were called first mention. Next, respondents were
asked, "What other area financial institutions are
you aware of?" The results were called other aware.
The sum of first mention and other aware was called
unaided awareness. Finally, of each of the banks
of interest not already mentioned, the respondents
were asked, "Are you at all aware of [bank]?" The
results were called aided awareness, and the sum of
unaided awareness and aided awareness was called
total awareness.

Based on the random market list base of 406
respondents, Table 1 presents the results for
selected financial institutions--those with an

awareness level or market share (See Table 2) of
at least 5 percent. Figure 1 shows the same results
graphically, but only for those banks where aided
awareness was sought.

Table 1

FINANCIAL INSTITUTION AWARENESS IN THE METROLAND MARKET
(Random Market List, N=406)

Selected Banks	First Mention	Other Aware	Unaided Awareness	Aided Awareness	Total Awareness
Dominant Trust Bank	22.7%	21.9%	44.6%	50.5%	95.1%
Evermore National Bank	7.6	16.7	24.4	67.0	91.4
Maturing Bank & Trust	12.1	16.7	28.8	56.4	85.2
Energetic Trust	4.4	9.9	14.3	62.6	76.8
Forest Banks (net)*	3.9	5.9	9.4	54.9	62.8
... of City A	3.4	4.2	7.6	54.9	62.6
... of City B	0.2	0.7	1.0	NA	1.0
... of City C	0.2	1.2	1.5	NA	1.5
... Unspecified	-	-	-	NA	-
FNB of Forest	2.5	6.9	9.4	58.6	68.0
Farmers Bank	2.2	5.4	7.6	43.8	51.5
Bank D	1.0	5.4	6.4	NA	6.4
Bank E	2.2	3.7	5.9	NA	5.9
Bank F	2.5	4.2	6.7	NA	6.7
Bank G	2.7	2.5	5.2	NA	5.2
Bank H	5.9	7.6	13.5	NA	13.5
Selected S&L's					
First State S&L	2.0	7.1	9.1	NA	9.1
Evermore Federal	0.7	1.7	2.5	NA	2.5
Upper Forest Federal	1.2	1.7	3.0	NA	3.0
Ficuciary Fidelity S&L	2.2	7.6	9.9	NA	9.9
Security Federal	2.0	5.7	7.6	NA	7.6
Credit Unions (net)*	2.0	3.2	5.9	NA	5.9

Note: Percentages will not always add across exactly because of rounding error.
Percentages may add up to more than 100.0% because of multiple mentions.

*Nets are unduplicated sums; therefore, the results of adding numbers in the
table will not always agree with sums in the table.

Figure 1

BANK AWARENESS IN THE METROLAND MARKET

Dominant Trust   =======23=======]----------22----------]   50   95
                                                                    45

Evermore Nat'l   ===8===]------17------]   67   91
                                24

Maturing B & T   ====12====]------17------]   56   85
                                29

Energetic Trust   =4=]----10---]   63   77
                        14

Forest Banks   =4=]--6--]   55   63
                      9

FNB of Forest   2]--7--]   59   68
                    9

Farmers Bank   2]--5--]   44   52
                    8

                  0   50   100

Key

=== First Mention

--- Other Aware

___ Aided Awareness

Notes

1. Percentages across may not add exactly due to rounding error.

2. The results for Forest Banks are based on the unduplicated sums of all individual Forest Banks; therefore, the total awareness percentage is less than the sum of unaided and aided awareness.

Dominant Trust was the dominant leader in both first mention and unaided awareness. While still the leader in total awareness, Dominant Trust's lead was narrower.

Energetic Trust was a distant fourth in first mention, unaided, and aided awareness. Second and third place changed between unaided and total awareness. Although Maturing Bank and Trust held a narrow lead for second place over Evermore National` in unaided awareness, Evermore National took second place in total awareness.

With the exception of customers of a bank tending to report higher awareness of their bank, an expected finding, the only statistically significant difference found in the crosstabulation review was a difference in first mention awareness between Oak Forest and Forest Village Counties, with the principal contributor to the difference being a higher awareness of Maturing Bank and Trust in Forest Village County (18.0 percent) than in Oak Forest County (6.3 percent).

Service Usage

Among the 406 respondents from the random market list, the incidence of service usage was:

NOW accounts	22.7 percent
Checking accounts	91.4 percent
CD's	34.5 percent
Savings accounts	91.1 percent
Money market funds	18.0 percent

Crosstabulation analysis revealed statistically significant differences in the incidence of service usage.

- NOW accounts were higher
  in these cases: Main
  Bank: noncustomer vs.
  Dominant Trust   (27.1% vs. 10.7%)
  More than high school:
  yes vs. no   (25.3% vs. 15.5%)
  College graduate or more:
  yes vs. no   (31.0% vs. 15.4%)
- Checking accounts were
  higher in these cases:
  Income: $25,000 or more
  vs. less than $25,000   (94.1% vs. 86.5%)
  Customer of Dominant Trust:
  yes vs. no   (95.9% vs. 91.1%)
- Certificates of deposit were
  higher in these cases:
  Age: 35 or more vs.
  under 35   (41.9% vs. 24.1%)

Income: $25,000 or more

vs. less than $25,000   (37.5% vs. 26.2%)

Years at current address:

5+ vs. less than 5   (43.0% vs. 25.1%)

Years lived in area: 15+

vs. less than 15   (37.6% vs. 22.8%)

Ownership: own vs. rent   (41.0% vs. 20.4%)

● Savings accounts were higher

in these cases: Age: 35

or more vs. under 35   (94.4% vs. 88.6%)

Ownership: own vs. rent   (95.1% vs. 84.4%)

● Money market funds were

higher in these cases:

College graduate or more:

yes vs. no   (25.4% vs. 12.9%)

Sex: male vs. female   (22.8% vs. 14.3%)

Married: yes vs. no   (21.5% vs. 11.3%)

Age: 35 or more vs.

under 35   (24.0% vs. 9.6%)

Income: $25,000 or more

vs. less than $25,000   (19.4% vs. 8.9%)

The incidence of service usage profiles above
can provide useful guidance in marketing services
already offered by Dominant Trust or in developing

a new product to compete with money market funds.

Market Shares

Each respondent who reported a CD, NOW,
checking, or savings account was asked at what
banks or savings and loans the respondent had the
account. In addition respondents were asked,
"Overall, which bank or S&L do you consider to be
your household's main or primary financial
institution?" Table 2 presents the results for
the same financial institutions used in Table 1 for
awareness.

As with awareness, Dominant Trust was the
market share leader in all categories, but for
second place and beyond the pattern is much less clear.

For main bank share the rank order was the
same for unaided awareness--Maturing Bank and Trust
in second, Evermore National in third, and Energetic
Trust in fourth place. For any account type,
Maturing Bank and Trust kept second place and
Evermore National kept third place, but First
State S&L replaced Energetic Trust in fourth place.

Maturing Bank and Trust was also in second
place for checking and savings, while Evermore National
kept third place in checking and slipped a place to fourth in

savings. Third place in savings went to First

State S&L,

Second and fourth place in NOW accounts went

Table 2

MARKET SHARES IN THE METROLAND MARKET

	Main Bank (N=406)	Any Account Type (N=406)	NOW (N=92)	By Account Type Checking (N=371)	CD's (N=140)	Saving (N=370
Selected Banks						
Dominant Trust Bank	20.9%	26.1%	12.0%	25.3%	15.0%	18.1%
Evermore National Bank	7.1	9.9	3.3	9.2	5.7	8.1
Maturing Bank & Trust	12.6	16.5	2.2	15.1	4.3	10.8
Energetic Trust	4.7	7.4	6.5	5.9	5.7	4.6
Forest Banks (net)*	2.5	5.7	2.2	4.0	1.4	3.0
... of City A	2.2	3.9	2.2	2.7	0.7	2.4
... of City B	-	0.7	-	0.8	-	-
... of City C	0.2	1.2	-	1.1	0.7	0.3
... Unspecified	-	0.5	-	0.3	-	0.3
FNB of Forest	2.7	4.2	1.1	2.7	3.6	2.7
Farmers Bank	3.2	4.2	3.3	4.0	2.1	2.2
Bank D	0.7	1.7	1.1	1.3	-	0.3
Bank E	3.0	4.2	1.1	4.3	1.4	1.6
Bank F	2.2	3.4	1.1	3.2	2.1	1.6
Bank G	3.7	4.4	-	4.9	-	1.9
Bank H	2.0	3.2	2.2	2.7	0.7	1.4
Selected S&L's						
First State S&L	1.5	8.6	-	0.5	5.0	8.4
Evermore Federal	1.0	3.9	5.4	0.5	5.7	3.0
Upper Forest Federal	0.7	3.0	7.6	1.1	3.6	1.6
Fiduciary Fidelity S&L	2.7	7.4	5.4	0.5	7.9	7.0
Security Federal	2.0	3.9	15.2	2.2	2.9	0.3
Credit Unions (net)*	3.7	8.9	6.5	2.4	5.7	8.9

Note: Percentages will not always add across exactly because of rounding error.
Percentages may add up to more than 100.0% because of multiple mentions.
Percentages in the Any Account Type column may be lower than corresponding percentages in the By Account Type columns because of a larger
denominator.

*Nets are unduplicated sums; therefore, the results of adding numbers in the
table will not always agree with sums in the table.

to S&Ls--Upper Forest Federal in second and Evermore
Federal and Fiduciary Fidelity tied for fourth. The
reporting of S&L checking accounts could be reclassi-
fied as NOW accounts, but the rank order results
would not change. Third place went to Energetic
Trust while Maturing Bank and Trust and Evermore
National, the two banks usually ahead of Energetic
Trust, fell behind.

Second place for CDs also went to a S&L,
Fiduciary Fidelity, while there was a tie for third
place among Evermore Federal, Evermore National,
and Energetic Trust.

Government credit unions as a group gained an
8.9 percent share of "any account type" and of
savings, making them an important factor in the
Metroland market.

As with awareness, crosstabulation analysis
revealed that Maturing Bank and Trust was
statistically stronger in market shares in Forest
Village County than in Oak Forest County:

Main bank	(17.0% versus 8.3%)
Any bank	(21.5% versus 11.7%)
Checking	(18.0% versus 9.8%)
Savings	(13.0% versus 6.8%)

There were not enough respondents to analyze
NOW accounts or certificates of deposit.

The only other statistically significant
difference found was for main bank share among
married people with and without dual incomes,
where Dominant Trust scored higher among those
without than among those with dual incomes (23.0
percent versus 18.8 percent), and Maturing Bank
and Trust scored higher among those with than among
those without dual incomes (14.1 percent versus 8.8
percent).

BEHAVIORAL CHARACTERISTICS

When respondents from the random market list
were asked about the location of the branch of their
main financial institution used most often, the
results were:

Closer to home	50.2 percent
Closer to work	22.4 percent
About the same	23.4 percent
Don't work/no answer	3.9 percent

Crosstabulation analysis revealed statistically
significant differences in banking closer to home or
work.

Banks Near Home

Sex: female vs. male	(78.9% vs. 60.1%)
Married: no vs. yes	(80.7% vs. 64.2%)
Years at current address:	
5+ vs. less than 5	(75.4% vs. 61.3%)
Years lived in area:	
15+ vs. less than 15	(73.2% vs. 47.8%)

Main Bank: Suburban

    Trust vs. noncustomer   (79.8% vs. 67.6%)

More than high school:

    no vs. yes   (84.7% vs. 63.4%)

College graduate or

    more: no vs. yes   (75.7% vs. 61.8%)

Banks Near Work

    Sex: male vs. female   (39.9% vs. 21.1%)

    Married: yes vs. no   (35.8% vs. 19.3%)

Years at current address:

    less than 5 vs. 5+   (38.7% vs. 24.6%)

Years lived in area:

    less than 15 vs. 15+   (52.2% vs. 26.8%)

Main Bank: noncustomer

    vs. Dominant Trust   (32.4% vs. 20.2%)

More than high school:

    yes vs. no   (36.6% vs. 15.3%)

College graduate or

    more: yes vs. no   (38.2% vs. 24.3%)

The profile of customers who bank near home can aid in developing programs to attract or retain residential customers in a branch trade area. Likewise, the profile of customers who bank near work can help when area workers are the target.

Switching Behavior

Respondents from the random market list were

asked, "In the past twelve months, for reasons other than moving your residence or changing jobs, did you switch to [main institution] from another financial institution in the area?" and the results were:

Yes   14.0 percent
No   86.0 percent

The 57 respondents who reported switching were asked: "Which one did you switch from?" Results for selected banks are reported below along with main bank share for comparison.

	Lost as Main Bank (N=57)	Have as Main Bank (N=4-6)
Dominant Trust	17.5%	20.9%
Evermore National	8.8%	7.1%
Maturing Bank and Trust	19.3%	12.6%
Energetic Trust	5.3%	4.7%

In comparison with the main bank shares, it appears that Dominant Trust lost fewer than would be expected, while the other three banks lost more than would be expected; however, the low number of responses does not make it possible to reach a firm conclusion.

DEMOGRAPHIC PROFILE CHARACTERISTICS
IN THE METROLAND MARKET

Table 3 shows the demographic profile of Dominant Trust customers and noncustomers. Of the nine characteristics, there were statistically

significant differences for three characteristics.
In comparison with competitors, Dominant Trust
attracted as customers people who:

- have lived at their current address
  longer, with an average duration of
  11.5 years versus 9.8 years;
- have lived in the Metroland area
  longer, with an average duration of
  21.9 years versus 17.6 years;
- are less likely to be married (64.1
  percent versus 73.1 percent) and more
  likely to be single, divorced,
  separated, or widowed (35.4 percent
  versus 24.9 percent).

No statistically significant differences were
found in dwelling ownership, incidence of dual
incomes among married people, education, household
size, age, or annual income.

In summary, the demographic profile of
Dominant Trust customers can be described as:

- Median current residence of 8.5 years
  and average of 11.5 years.
- Median Metroland residence of 22.0
  years and average of 21.9 years.
- Seven in ten owners and three in ten
  renters.

- Among married people, almost two-thirds with dual incomes.

- Also two-thirds married and one-third not married.

- Three-fourths having some college or more, with about one-fourth having some graduate school or more.

- Median household size of 3.2 and average of 3.0.

- Median age of 42.6 years and average of 43.8 years.

- Median annual household income of $29,400 and average of $33,000.

Table 3

DEMOGRAPHIC PROFILE CHARACTERISTICS
IN METROLAND MARKET

	Market Area	Dominant Trust Customer Yes	Dominant Trust Customer No
Duration of Current Residence**	(N=401)	(N=195)	(N=300)
0-0.9 years	9.5%	7.7%	10.3%
1-2.9	19.5	15.9	20.3
3-4.9	16.0	12.8	17.0
5-9.9	18.0	19.5	17.0
10-14.9	11.0	10.3	12.3
15-19.9	9.2	11.8	8.0
20-24.9	6.2	13.8	3.7
25 or more	10.6	8.2	11.4
Mean (years)	10.3	11.5	9.8
Median (years)	6.4	8.5	5.7
Duration of Metroland Residence*	(N=401)	(N=195)	(N=300)
0-0.9	2.2%	1.5%	2.7%
1-2.9	4.2	6.7	5.0
3-4.9	8.2	3.6	9.7
5-9.9	14.5	9.2	15.7
10-14.9	14.7	10.8	15.7
15-19.9	13.2	11.3	13.7
20-24.9	13.0	16.9	11.3
25-29.9	9.0	11.3	8.0
30-39.9	12.2	16.4	10.0
40 or more	8.7	12.3	8.3
Mean (years)	18.8	21.9	17.6
Median (years)	17.3	22.0	15.5
Dwelling Ownership	(N=406)	(N=195)	(N=305)
Own	71.2	69.7%	70.2%
Rent	27.3	30.3	27.9
Refused	1.5	-	2.0

*Statistically significant difference between Dominant Trust customers and noncustomers.

.**Statistically significant difference between Dominant Trust customers and noncustomers on the basis of Chi-square analysis but no statistically significant difference on the basis of the T-test.

Continued . . .

Table 3 (continued)

DEMOGRAPHIC PROFILE CHARACTERISTICS
IN THE METROLAND MARKET

	Market Area	Dominant Trust Customer Yes	No
Married with Dual Income	(N=289)	(N=125)	(N=223)
Yes	58.8%	63.2%	56.5%
No	38.8	36.0	40.4
No answer/refused	2.4	0.8	3.1
Marital Status*	(N=406)	(N=195)	(N=305)
Married	71.2%	64.1%	73.1%
Not married	27.1	35.4	24.9
Refused	1.7	0.5	2.0
Education	(N=406)	(N=195)	(N=305)
Less than high school (10)	3.2%	4.1%	3.0%
High school graduate (12)	22.2	25.6	20.7
Some college (14)	25.9	22.6	24.9
College graduate (16)	22.2	22.1	22.3
Some graduate school (18)	7.1	6.2	8.5
Completed graduate school (20)	17.0	19.0	17.7
Don't know/no answer	2.5	0.5	3.0
Mean (years)	15.2	15.2	15.4
Median (years)	15.9	15.7	16.1
Household Size	(N=397)	(N=192)	(N=297)
One	13.1%	14.6%	12.1%
Two	36.0	31.2	36.4
Three	18.1	20.3	18.9
Four	19.9	19.8	19.5
Five	7.1	4.7	8.4
Six or more	5.7	9.4	4.7
Mean	2.95	3.02	2.95
Median	3.05	3.21	3.08

*Statistically significant difference between Dominant Trust
customers and noncustomers.

Continued . . .

Table 3 (continued)

DEOMOGRAPHIC PROFILE CHARACTERISTICS
IN THE METROLAND MARKET

	Market Area	Dominant Trust Customer	
		Yes	No
Age	(N=401)	(N=194)	(N=300)
Under 35	37.2%	36.6%	38.0%
35-54	38.2	34.0	39.0
55 or older	24.7	29.4	23.0
Mean (years)	43.5	43.8	43.2
Median (years)	41.1	42.6	40.5
Annual Household Income	(N=307)	(N=152)	(N=224)
Less than $ 25,000	33.9%	40.1%	31.2%
$ 25,000 or more	66.1	59.9	68.7
Mean	$35,200	$33,000	$36,000
Median	$30,800	$29,400	$31,600

Note: The market area column was based on the random market list;
the next two columns were based on that list plus the
Dominant Trust list. Percentages may not all add up to
exactly 100.0% because of rounding error.

BANK IMAGE PROFILES

IN THE METROLAND MARKET

Multiple Regression,

Image Profile, and Gap Analysis

The detailed image profile presented in this
section can be understood better with the benefit
of brief descriptions of multiple regression, how
bank awareness and image work together, and the
concept of gap analysis.

Multiple regression is a statistical tool
used to identify the image attributes most important

in _predicting_ the overall rating of a bank.

In this study, "A good place to do business with" was used as the overall rating and was called the dependent variable. The other thirteen attributes were used to predict the dependent variable and were called the independent variables. Separate multiple regressions were performed for Dominant Trust, Evermore National, and Maturing Bank and Trust. Each multiple regression proceeded in a stepwise fashion as follows.

Imagine 13 separate two-dimensional graphs, one for each of the thirteen independent variables plotted separately against the single dependent variable. The points could form the following kinds of shapes if a line were drawn to surround them:

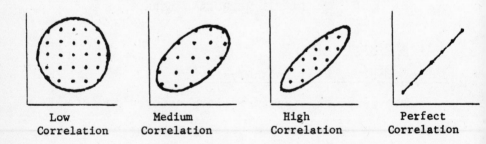

| Low
Correlation | Medium
Correlation | High
Correlation | Perfect
Correlation |

The first step of multiple regression involved selecting the two-dimensional graph with the longest and narrowest pattern of dots and then representing those dots with the best possible

straight line (one-dimensional), called a <u>least</u>
<u>squares regression line</u>:

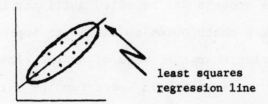

least squares
regression line

The graph selected identified the first
independent variable in the multiple regression.

Similarly, the second step of multiple
regression looked at twelve (not thirteen) three-
dimensional graphs, one for each of the twelve
remaining independent variables plotted separately
against the dependent variable, <u>and</u> the independent
variable already in the multiple regression. The
graph with the longest, narrowest, and thinnest
clump of dots was selected and represented by the
best possible plane (two-dimensional). The graph
selected identified the second independent variable
in the multiple regression as that single attribute
that added most to correlation with (or prediction
of) the dependent variable.

Similarly, the third step looked at the eleven
remaining independent variables and found the best
possible cube (three-dimensional). It is not
possible visually to graph beyond three dimensions;

however, multiple regression deals conceptually in multidimensional space.

The process was repeated until the remaining attributes contributed so little to improving correlation that they were of no practical importance.

It is essential in understanding multiple regression to remember that <u>high correlation is not necessarily good</u>. High correlation says that one attribute is good at predicting another. A high score by a respondent on one attribute predicts a high score on another, <u>and</u> a low score predicts a low score.

Before customers or potential customers can have an image of a bank, they must at least be aware of the bank. Building awareness is the first order of business, and awareness may be communicated through the use of image attributes that set the bank apart from competition.

Image attributes can be classified into four groups:

1. <u>Basic attributes</u>. These are givens in the marketplace. They are attributes that customers expect any bank to exhibit. Poor performance can spell disaster, but good performance doesn't necessarily offer a competitive

edge. Basic attributes are those that have high mean scores for the ideal bank but do not appear at the end of the list of image attributes in the multiple regressions.

2. Primary attributes. These are the image attributes at the top of the regression analysis. Assuming that there is no deficiency on basic attributes, the comparison of primary attributes across banks identifies who has a competitive edge where.

3. Double primary attributes. These are primary attributes that are high in our multiple regression but low in the multiple regressions of competitors. Double primary attributes identify more than just a narrow competitive edge

4. Secondary attributes. These are the image attributes that are neither basic nor primary. After taking advantage of competitive edges resulting from primary attributes, taking advantage of secondary

attributes makes for an even stronger
competitive position.

Gap Analysis

Gap analysis refers to placing image attributes
in rank order according to the ideal bank and then
inspecting the most important attributes to see
whether a bank ranks substantially higher or lower
than competitors. The identification of image gaps
can be used in advertising and other communications
with the marketplace to position the bank according
to desired image attributes.

All of these concepts are additive. Each
step augments and reinforces the step before, and
every step must be sure before the next one can be
taken. Here's the sequence.

1. Gain high levels of awareness.
2. Be sure there are no problems with
   image on basic attributes.
3. Leverage competitive advantages on
   primary attributes, especially any
   double primary attributes.
4. Leverage competitive advantages on
   secondary attributes and/or image
   gaps.

Figure 2

BANK IMAGE PROFILES IN THE METROLAND MARKET

	1	2	3	4	5
Makes few errors					
Convenient location					
Convenient business hours					
Highest interest on savings					
Fast service					
Low service charges					
Helpful personnel					
Friendly personnel					
A good place to get a loan					
Gives good financial advice					
Has many branches					
Has 24-hour teller machines					
First to offer new services					

—— Ideal Bank   --- Evermore National
*** Dominant Trust   ∘∘∘ Maturing B & T

CONCLUSIONS AND RECOMMENDATIONS

In the area of awareness, the first step in getting a customer, Dominant Trust enjoys first position in the market. To reinforce that dominant image the bank should continue its aggressive communications program with the marketplace. The content of those communications should be based on the findings of this study.

Specialized Markets

Dominant Trust operates in a large, homogeneous market where important submarkets with different image profiles requiring specialized target market programs do not exist. Therefore, Dominant Trust should adopt a competitive positioning stance against the marketplace as a whole.

Friendly, Low-Cost Bank

We should communicate and make believable the image we already have as the friendly, low-cost bank. The idea is that we should do a good job where we are already strong and avoid losing our existing franchise as we augment our attack with the next recommendation.

Helpful Bank

We should position Dominant Trust as helpful to counteract the most important image attribute of competitors. Since "friendly personnel" and "helpful personnel" were highly intercorrelated, our efforts in positioning the bank as friendly should go a long way toward attacking the strength of the competition. In addition, the current advertising campaign that positions Dominant Trust as the friendly helpmate in fighting inflation should add extra punch.

A Good Place to Get a Loan

Dominant Trust should position itself as a good place to get a loan to counteract Evermore National's second most important attribute. In other studies we have found that, as long as a bank is rate competitive, augmenting its image as friendly and competent also improves its image as a good place to get a loan. We could communicate this message with both deposit situation and loan situation ads.

Fast Service

To meet other competitive strengths, we should position Dominant as offering fast service. Fast service was ranked second in Maturing Bank and Trust's image profile and was Evermore National's third most important attribute. The long-term goal of this and the preceding three recommendations should be both to communicate and to make believable by word and deed that Dominant Trust has friendly, helpful personnel who make loans, offer services at low charges, and operate in a fast, efficient (with few errors) manner.

Few Errors

We should take advantage of the image gap that exists in "makes few errors in customer accounts," not only by working to control the actual error rate (a matter of measurable fact) but also by improving the way customers are treated when errors are found. Other studies have shown that the rating of errors is not related to the error itself but to how the error is handled by our staff. If our personnel are friendly and helpful in correcting the error, and if the customer receives a written and oral apology, he is usually satisfied. People expect errors, but they expect them to be corrected in an efficient and courteous manner.

Advertising Direction

The findings of this study should be used to guide all our advertising efforts, particularly in the following areas:

- Media selection should be based on targeting of special groups for improvement of selected attributes.

- Our customer base should be expanded by seeking to attract newer people to the area while not alienating our current customer base.

- Differences in demographic profiles of customers who bank near home versus those who bank near work should be used to develop advertising campaigns to attract branch bank customers.

- The service usage demographic profiles should be used as a guide to marketing current services or developing new services to compete with money market funds.

A Final Note

This was an extensive study, and the findings reinforced our belief that Dominant Trust is the market leader. If the information is used properly and the recommendations followed, we are confident we can improve our already dominant market share.

15

Reports—Miscellaneous Problems

". . . the more rapidly changing and novel the environment, the more information the individual needs to process in order to make effective rational decisions."

Alvin Toffler

It has been said again and again that business operates on information, and in today's high technology world the old axiom is especially appropriate.

Probably the report writer's single greatest challenge in the modern information maze is to get the intended audience to read the report. The second greatest challenge may well be to get the reader to believe the report once he has read and understood it.

Throughout this book, and especially in this section on report writing, I have attempted to identify readability characteristics, to offer suggestions for improvement, and to emphasize the importance of precision, accuracy, and thoroughness in establishing credibility with the reader.

PRIORITIES AND PAGE HEADINGS

The outline in the example presented in the previous chapter illustrates how the findings or central messages of the report govern its final layout. The most important information to be reported on is included in the topic outline and quite naturally corresponds with page headings in the final report. Supporting information about each topic is added to expand the outline and provide a smooth transition between related thoughts of the same general concept.

Again, using the outline as a guide, the page is designed around the main and subheadings. The main heading is centered and capitalized while the subheadings are flush left, using uppercase and lowercase letters, and are underlined. Such graphic treatment tells the reader visually that information contained under less dominant forms of headings support the main heading.

This presentation is a form of visual shorthand that guides the reader from point to point without having to read every word on the page. However, the information should be complete so that when the reader does need all the details they are there.

I once had a client who would not permit me to write complete descriptions of his product in the literature. He said "Nobody ever reads all that stuff, anyway. Just list the key features in bullet point form."

While it is true that a great number of people do not read "all that stuff," studies have shown that a substantial number of readers of direct mail pieces, for example, need more persuasion than a bullet point listing of the key product features. It is for their benefit that the detailed descriptions are included.

The same is true for readers of your reports. There are those who will skim the page headings and read a little of the supporting information, form opinions, and make decisions based on that skimpy amount of information. Others need more information to be convinced, and in a situation in which the merits of your recommendations are being discussed the thoughtful information seekers will usually prevail over those who skim the report and "wing it" in the meeting. The point: make the headings leap off the page at the reader; make it easy to skim, and visually pleasing; but make sure the report is complete. .

Another important consideration in the finished presentation of the report is to make sure it is parallel both in appearance and in construction. If you use side headings for subordinate information in one section of the report, use the same arrangement in all other sections to facilitate the reader's instant comprehension.

Parallel construction here refers to the balance of the entire report. The areas that are most important are those to which you should devote the greatest amount of time and space. Scan the report in both the outline and early draft stages to make sure your emphasis is placed properly.

REPORT COVERS AND GRAPHICS

In report writing, use graphics whenever possible to illustrate your message. We are able to understand complicated concepts much more readily when we see the whole picture and relationships between various elements of the information being presented. If you doubt this concept, test yourself the next time you buy something unassembled. If you are like most people, you look at the illustrations and schematics first; then, when all else fails, you read the directions.

The illustrations and graphics need not be elaborate or sophisticated. Their sole purpose is to facilitate the transmission of information. In Chapter 7 there are several examples of how to make charts, graphs, and tables quickly and easily by using rub-off or transfer lettering and symbols. These letters and symbols can be supplemented with typewritten or hand-drawn information, as demonstrated in the sample report presented in the previous chapter.

Transfer letters and symbols are effective for the production of report covers as well, or you may prefer to develop a standard report cover for multiple uses that allows space for inserting the typewritten title of individual reports.

If your firm has a graphics department, the staff artists can design a special cover for you, or a multiple-use cover, as you prefer. If not, a free-lance commercial artist offers similar types of services. (Refer to Chapter 7 for suggestions in purchasing graphics services.)

For simple report covers you may elect to do the work yourself, using transfer lettering and symbols, hand-drawn sketches, typewritten information, or a combination of any or all of these alternatives. Or you may eschew all the embellishments and simply type the title of the report and other pertinent information. The choice is yours.

EXECUTIVE SUMMARIES

If your report is ten pages or longer, it is generally considered a long report. As such, it should include an executive summary. Again, some report writers argue that executive summaries discourage readers from reading the entire report. I doubt that assumption is true. If anything, the executive summary should pique the reader's interest and pull him into the rest of the report. In worst-case situations, when the reader does read the summary only, it is still better than him reading only a portion of the report and making a decision based on incomplete information. An executive summary is a "no lose" addition to any report.

The information that should be included in the executive summary is left to the discretion of the writer. A good practice to follow is to extract only the most important findings and recommendations for the executive summary to keep it brief and to arouse the reader's desire to know more about the subject.

TRANSMITTAL MEMOS

Whether to use a transmittal memo or not is usually left to the author of the report as well, but it is generally a good idea. Even if it says nothing more than "Here is your copy of the final report," it serves as a formal notice that the report is complete and reminds recipients who sent it. In addition, many executives use a follow-up system based on filing memos according to the date they plan to check to see if the appropriate action was taken regarding your recommendations. Make it easy for them to check on your recommendations—use a transmittal memo.

More important, however, the transmittal memo provides a vehicle for you to tell the reader something about your report in a more informal way. Use this opportunity to sell your reader on the value of the information contained in it, and encourage him to read certain key portions that may be the most interesting and important.

TABLE OF CONTENTS

If your report is ten or more pages in length, use a table of contents. After you have completed the report, go through it and list the primary and secondary headings in order of appearance and list the pages on which they appear. (Refer to the sample report in the previous chapter for an example of how headings and subheadings were converted to a table of contents.)

In very long reports you may wish to expand the table of contents so that it is more descriptive and highlights topical information within subsections of the report.

If you are in doubt as to whether or not to include a table of contents, use one. Very little effort is required to produce it, and it will most likely be beneficial to the reader.

TAB DIVIDERS

In longer reports separating sections can be facilitated through the use of tab dividers organized according to main headings listed in the table of contents. Such dividers allow the reader to turn immediately to the section he wants. Tabs provide another opportunity to make it easy for your reader.

The physical construction of tabs may vary substantially. Simple dividers may be made from construction paper, cover stock, or any heavier paper and tabbed using typewritten legends inserted in plastic sleeves with self-adhesive flaps that attach to the divider. These are commercially available in office supply and stationery stores and through office supply mail order firms.

Another simple tab divider can be made by cutting a regular file folder at the fold and typing the legend on pressure-sensitive labels designed for use on file folders.

More elaborate dividers can be die cut to the shape you wish and printed by a commerical printer. At your option your printer can overlay a protective plastic material on the tab portion. If you use a large quantity of dividers on a regular basis, you may wish to ask your printer to die cut several varieties of tab dividers and store them for imprinting as needed. This substantially shortens the preparation time.

NOTES

If you use secondary (published) information in your report, you should document the source of that information in a note.

Your decision to use source notes should be based on two primary considerations: (1) giving credit where credit is due and (2) lending the support of authority to the information.[1]

Even if you decide to rewrite published information in your own words, you should note the source, unless the information is common knowledge in your business profession. That decision is yours, but it is a simple matter to include the reference. If you are uncertain about whether to note or not, you probably should do so.

Initially, handling notes seemed to be some sort of puzzle that I could never quite solve. When I finally understood that source notes and bibliographies are arranged differently, even though they contain the same information, I began to solve the puzzle. Let's look at source notes first. All notes should contain the following information.

- *The author's name.* It is not necessary to alphabetize notes, since notes appear in numerical, not alphabetical, order. However, since the author's name will be alphabetized in the bibliography, you may want to list them with last name first in your notes for convenience in alphabetizing later.
- *The complete title of the publication.* If it is a book, include all subtitles. Capitalize all words in the title except articles and short conjunctions. Italicize or underline all words in the title.
- *The title of the article.* If your source of information is a reference other than a book, such as a magazine, newspaper, encyclopedia, or almanac, the article title should be placed in quotation marks and the name of the publication italicized or underlined.

In Text Example

In recent years some authors have elected to include source note information in the text, eliminating the need for footnotes or a note section at the end of the document.

```
      Suzette Haden Elgin says that charismatic

speech is always balanced speech.  That balance

makes it easy to listen and remember.  It makes
```

following the speaker something you can do without effort, because you so quickly catch on to the pattern and know what to expect.   (The Gentle Art of Verbal Self-Defense [Englewood Cliffs, NJ: Prentice-Hall, Inc., 1980], p. 223.)

Footnote Example

Footnotes should be single-spaced with double-spacing between notes. Notes should be separated from the page of text by two spaces and a solid line fifteen spaces long beginning at the left-hand margin.[2] The first line of the footnote should be indented, with footnote numbers typed above the line. The previous example, if it appeared as a footnote, would be as follows.

[1]Suzette Haden Elgin, The Gentle Art of Verbal Self-Defense. (Englewood Cliffs, NJ: Prentice-Hall, Inc., 1980), p. 223.

End of Document Notes

Notes that appear at the end of your work, whether it is a report or a book, are arranged in the same order as footnotes except that there is no need for a fifteen-space solid line to separate notes from the text. Single-space the notes and double-space between them.

Magazine Example

The principal difference between magazines, newspapers, etc., and books is that you need to identify the title of the article by placing it in quotes. A note identifying a magazine article would appear as follows.

[9]Alan Anderson, "Neurotoxic Follies," Psychology Today, July 1982, p. 30.

BIBLIOGRAPHY

The bibliography contains the same information as that in the footnotes but in a slightly different order. The references used in the previous examples would appear in the bibliography as follows.

Anderson, Alan. "Neurotoxic Follies," <u>Psychology</u> <u>Today</u>.
     July 1982, p. 30-42.

Elgin, Suzette Haden. <u>The</u> <u>Gentle</u> <u>Art</u> <u>of</u> <u>Verbal</u>
     <u>Self-Defense</u>. Englewood Cliffs, NJ: Prentice-
     Hall, Inc., 1980.

Entries in the bibliography begin flush left with subsequent lines indented five spaces in a hanging indentation form. Bibliography entries are alphabetized within the separate categories of publications, such as books, magazines and periodicals, etc.

SECOND REFERENCES

If you want to save both yourself and your reader a lot of aggravation in second footnote references, follow the example of the Catholic Church and do away with the Latin. If the Church which views change as something that happens over a period of centuries now conducts Mass in English, modern business writers should do the same with second footnote references. Instead of *op cit* and *ibid,* use the author's last name or an abbreviated version of the title and the page number. The examples used previously in the second usage would appear as follows.

     Elgin, p. 225.

EXHIBITS AND APPENDICES

The purpose of exhibits and appendices is to provide a home for information that may be pertinent to the topic but is too lengthy, complex, or detailed to be included in the text. Computer printouts, related articles, tables, complicated computations, work papers, and other sources of documentation are examples of the kind of information typically included in appendices.

There is no reliable rule of thumb for what should and should not be included in an appendix. If, as you are assembling the data for the report, you frequently use one particular source of infor-

236 WRITING EFFECTIVE BUSINESS LETTERS

mation, that document might be helpful to readers. Or, if one point or another needs supporting documentation to assure credibility, you may want to include the appropriate work papers or other backup information. The choice is up to you; however, in this case fewer appendices are probably better than more. If you have more information in the back than you have in the report, your reader may wonder if you are sending a report or a clipping file.

16

Business Memoranda

"All writing is communication; creative writing is communication through revelation—it is the self escaping into the open. No writer long remains incognito."

Strunk and White

Just as every person has a unique personality, every piece of correspondence has attributes that the reader likes or dislikes. The best way to get the reader on your side right away is to be tactful and courteous in the opening sentence and continue that tone throughout.

As an example, let's assume that you are in charge of ordering supplies for your company. You have a request to check prices and availability of personalized stationery for one of the vice-presidents and report back to him in a memo. Maybe you don't agree with the idea and think it is a waste of the company's money when you already have perfectly good stationery in stock for everyone to use. Should your opinion be expressed subtly through the tone of your memo? Absolutely not. If you disagree with the decision and it is within your province to make such recommendations, say exactly what you mean. Don't leave it up to the reader to interpret your message.

237

Here are two ways to write the memo.

Wrong:

Per your request, we have checked prices for personalized stationery for corporate officers and find them to be exorbitant compared to what we pay for standard stationery that we have in stock and that has been approved for corporate use.

Right:

Thank you for your request that the supply department investigate the purchase of personalized stationery for corporate officers.

We have reviewed your requirements with our regular suppliers and obtained the following quotations:

	500	1,000
Letterheads	$ 34.95	$ 47.95
Envelopes	44.95	59.95
Second Sheets	15.95	28.95
	$ 95.85	$136.85

To supply each of our thirteen corporate officers with 1,000 letterheads, envelopes, and second sheets, the total cost would be $1,799.05. This compares to $693.45 for 1,000 letterheads, envelopes and second sheets of our current stationery.

In addition to cost considerations, a change to personalized stationery would require a policy change, as outlined in our corporate identification

manual (copy attached).

　　In view of the additional costs involved and

our current corporate policy, I recommend that we

continue to stock only the standard stationery for

office use.

　　Please let me know if you would like additional

information, or if I can be of further assistance.

Analysis: In this instance both memos convey essentially the same information but in a decidedly different manner. In the second example courtesy throughout keeps the reader focused on your message—not on the way you present it—and detailed information presented in an easily understandable format helps the reader reach a decision. In addition, you make an extra effort and outline the pertinent corporate policy. All these elements comprise the personality of your memo, and all will have some influence on how your reader reacts to your message.

Courtesy and positive tone are not to be confused with unnecessary small talk, which has no place in business correspondence of any type. If you plan to pass the time of day, do so after work. Don't waste your time, your typist's time, and your reader's time with specious comments in a memo.

Always present your message in a straightforward, positive, pleasant manner. Even bad news is more palatable if it is presented directly and courteously. Before you write, take a few minutes to anticipate how your reader might react to your message. Is he expecting your memo because he requested information, or are you sending it cold? An unexpected memo will probably require more background and explanation.

Are you presenting good news or bad news? If your message is favorable, the tone of the correspondence can easily be cheery. But what if the reverse is true? How do you tell the reader the bad news? Do you toss him a crumb of good news, then hit him between the eyes with the bad news?

The best approach to telling the bad news is to be direct. Get down to business right away. Don't keep your reader guessing or mislead him with a pleasant writing style. Here is an example.

Wrong:

The executive committee was most impressed with your analysis of our expected sales of #303 latex base paint and your corresponding capital equipment request for expanding the Des Moines manufacturing facility to accommodate the increased demand.

Our company has always prided itself on being a leader in the field in providing both innovative marketing techniques and state-of-the-art products to our customers. We have been able to do so by hiring the best people and giving them the financial and human resources necessary to get the job done.

The thoroughness with which you approached the task you were assigned indicates that we made the right choice by giving you this assignment. You have a bright future with the company.

Unfortunately, at this time we will be unable to grant your request for expansion of the sales force and the manufacturing facility.

Right:

The executive committee has carefully considered your request for expansion of the

Des Moines plant and sales force to accommodate
the expected increase in demand for our #303
latex base paint. Unfortunately, we cannot grant
your request at this time.

   Because of the high cost of borrowing money
and the uncertain economy, the executive committee
generally has postponed all capital expansion for
at least two years. Please resubmit your request
at that time.

   We were impressed with the thoroughness of
your analysis and consider you a valued asset to
the company. Keep up the good work.

Analysis: In the first example, building up the reader in the
beginning makes him feel he has been tricked when he finally
reaches the point at which you give him the bad news. Make sure
the portions of the message are weighted toward the total message. Spend more time on specific reasons for denying the request
rather than on what a terrific analysis he did.

Using specific words is only one way to keep the personality of
your memo pleasing and positive. Some others are:

- Emphasize results and benefits.
- Remember the reader's viewpoint.
- Keep your message simple and direct.
- Use an active and personal sentence structure.
- Avoid shifts in tone.
- Limit the memo to one topic.
- Avoid sexist language.
- Be realistic.

The choice of words is up to the writer, and the words you

select will have a substantial influence on how your reader perceives your message. For a list of positive and negative words to watch for, see Chapter 2.

ORGANIZATION AND FORMAT OF MEMORANDA

In large companies corporate policy handbooks or correspondence guides may outline the format to be followed for memos. Some preprint memo stationery, whereas others leave it to the discretion of the writer. Some are formal, whereas others are casual. There are probably as many different forms as there are companies, and all may be acceptable. When in doubt, however, follow these guidelines:

1. If it is important enough to write a memo about, it is important enough to be serious. Don't be flippant.
2. Don't use trendy words or jargon. Your memo may be on file as a reference for years to come.
3. Don't say anything in a memo that you wouldn't want the entire company to know about.
4. Don't say anything directly or indirectly that might embarrass the recipient.
5. A good memo should follow the rules for good letter writing. Each should contain:
   • a salutation,
   • identification of the subject matter,
   • introduction of the idea,
   • main body of the message, and
   • a call for action.
6. Memoranda should be visually pleasing. If you do not have a corporate format, use one of the following.

MEMORANDUM

To:	L. E. Jones	Date:	September 1, 19xx
Office:	Memphis	Steno:	JP
From:	S. A. Cypert	Enc:	Agenda
Office:	Chicago	cc:	J. P. Smith
			New York

Subject: Plant Managers' Meeting

The annual division managers' meeting will be held

this year on November 1, 19xx, at the Peachtree
Hyatt in Atlanta, Georgia. Please refer to the
hotel's daily events listing for the meeting room
assigned to our company.

Please be prepared to give a twenty-minute presentation on your successful use of quality circles to
reduce manufacturing downtime. An agenda detailing
the complete program and your portion of it is
attached.

I am looking forward to seeing you again and am
most interested in your report.

Best wishes.

                        MEMORANDUM

TO: L. E. Jones   DATE: September 1, 19xx
       Memphis

FROM: S. A. Cypert   SUBJECT: Plant Managers'
       Chicago   Meeting

     The annual division managers' meeting will be
held this year on November 1, 19xx, at the Peachtree
Hyatt in Atlanta, Georgia. Please refer to the
hotel's daily events listing for the meeting room
assigned to our company.

     Please be prepared to give a twenty-minute
presentation on your successful use of quality
circles to reduce manufacturing downtime. An
agenda detailing the complete program and your
portion of it is attached.

     I am looking forward to seeing you again and
am most interested in your report.

     Best wishes.

SAC:JP
Enclosure--Agenda

cc: J. P. Smith--New York

MEMORANDUM

TO: L. E. Jones
      Memphis

FROM: S. A. Cypert
      Chicago

SUBJECT: Plant Managers'   DATE: September 1, 19xx
          Meeting

The annual division managers' meeting will be held
this year on November 1, 19xx, at the Peachtree
Hyatt in Atlanta, Georgia. Please refer to the
hotel's daily events listing for the meeting room
assigned to our company.

Please be prepared to give a twenty-minute presentation on your successful use of quality circles to
reduce manufacturing downtime. An agenda detailing
the complete program and your portion of it is
attached.

I am looking forward to seeing you again and am most
interested in your report.

Best wishes.

SAC:JC
cc: J. P. Smith--New York

Enclosure--Agenda

TYPES OF MEMORANDA

As with most written communications, memos are to some
degree informative, expressive, directive, or a combination of the
three. In one memo there may be information about the subject,
an opinion about how the problem should be handled, and
instructions for implementing the necessary corrective actions. In
addition to these general categories, specific types of memos can
be divided into the following classifications.

• Confirming memos are used to formalize a verbal agreement

or assignment to make sure that all parties involved understand the terms and conditions of the agreement of assignment (see Example 1).

- Follow-up memos serve as a reminder that a deadline or completion date is approaching (or has passed) (see Example 2).
- Courtesy memos express appreciation for a job well done or thank an associate for visiting your office or plant or for assisting in a project (see Example 3).
- Transmittal memos accompany reports, proposals, or other longer documents and may contain short summaries of key points (see Example 4).
- Standardized memos such as agendas, minutes, conference memos, and some types of instructional memos require no explanation other than what they are. The material contained in them should be self-explanatory (see Examples 5-8). (See Chapters 12-15 for more information about reports.)
- Informative memos are often distributed to large groups and are used to announce recent or future events. Examples would include transfers, promotions, fire safety information, approved holidays and the like (see Example 9).
- Directive memos are used to issue instructions about a variety of topics. They usually deal with matters of company policy such as record keeping, expense reports, office hours, or compliance with various rules and regulations (see Example 10).
- Memo reports are usually short, informal reports about a relatively simple topic. Typically, memo reports include identifying information about the sender and receiver, then report the information with little fanfare (see Example 11). (Chapters 12-15 contain more information about reports.)

Example 1

```
To:      V. P. Miller          April 11, 19xx
From:    P. D. Quicke
```

The final proof for the Personnel Manual (with corrections) was delivered to the printer April 9,

and delivery of the finished copies is expected
April 22.

As we discussed on Monday, because of the increased
number of pages, the costs will exceed the anticipated
budget. A comparison is listed below.

	Budget	Revised Estimate	Over (Under)	Percent
Typesetting	$ 3,200	$ 3,800	$ 600	18.7%
Printing	7,500	9,000	1,500	20 %
Misc. (Mailing services and proofreading)	1,800	1,123	(677)	38 %
Postage	1,500	4,740	3,240	216 %
	$14,000	$18,663	$4,663	33 %

As you can see, postage accounts for the largest
overage. We weighed a sample manual made from the
paper stock we will be using, as well as a transmittal memo and envelope to estimate postage costs.
The package metered at $1.58 for first-class mailing.

Our only variable is postage; the book could be
mailed third class (a savings of about $1,800),
which would result in a net overage of 14 percent.
As we discussed, the disadvantage is that third-
class mail takes about three to four weeks for
delivery.

We are proceeding with production and will mail
first class unless otherwise instructed, but I
thought you would like to see the revised numbers,
especially since the overage is greater than the
10-20 percent that I originally estimated.

Please let me know if you would like additional
information.

Example 2

To: R. Ashley   March 13, 19xx

From: A. Samuelson

Subject: Energy Industry Newsletter

Following our discussion a few weeks ago, I asked
our editorial and graphics department to give me

some suggestions on how the Energy Industry Newsletter might be improved. We all agree that it is
well done but believe our experience in national
newsletters could enable us to offer some helpful
suggestions.

I am attaching the editorial recommendations for
your review and four optional mastheads, each
with the front page completed, to demonstrate some
suggested graphic treatments.

We are still interested in working with you on
this newsletter should the opportunity arise. I
will call you next week to discuss this with you.

Example 3

To: Communications Department   October 2, 19xx

From: S. Cubar

Subject: Annual Report

On Wednesday (10-1-xx) I spoke with the president
of the Savings Bank, who approved the final copy
for the annual report. He asked that the 20,000
copies for mailing be shipped to them on Friday
(10-3-xx). The bank plans on mailing the annual
reports on Saturday (10-4-xx).

Ralph also expressed his satisfaction with the
report--he is very pleased with it. He thanked
us for our help in putting out the report in such
a short time.

I also thank everyone who worked on producing the
report. It looks great.

Example 4

To: N. T. Roberts   August 19, 19xx

From: F. E. Kennedy

Subject: Reinforced Plastics Market

Attached is a copy of a recently completed Market
Study on the reinforced plastics market. This

report specifically details the reinforced plastics
market segments of BMC (bulk molding compound) and
SMC (sheet molding compound).

The study reveals some areas of opportunity for
our company; however, at present the dollar
potential seems small. I would suggest you read
the study and familiarize yourself with the market.
As more information becomes available, and we
develop a marketing approach, I will forward the
information to you.

Example 5

COMMUNITY
CORPORATION
P.O. BOX 265
LAKE ZURICH, IL 60047

AGENDA

Board of Directors Meeting
June 18, 19xx
Community Center
8:00 p.m.

```
Call to Order........................ Skip Cypert
Reading of Minutes of Last Meeting... Peg Deutchman
Reports
     Treasurer....................... Karen Neubarth
     Vice-President.................. Diane Henkle
     Lake Commissioner.............. John Ryan
     Park Commissioner.............. John Leavy
     Streets and Sanitation
     Commissioner................. Howard Vasey
```

Old Business:

Pathways and easements
Cleanup of center

New Business:

Door-to-door soliciting
Purchasing procedures

Next Meeting Date:

July 13, 19xx

Example 6

COMMUNITY
CORPORATION
P.O. BOX 265
LAKE ZURICH, IL 60047

<u>Minutes</u>
Board of Directors Meeting
June 18, 19xx

The Meeting was convened by President
Skip Cypert at 8:00 p.m. in the
Community Center. Members present
were:

Skip Cypert	Diane Henkel
Howard Vassey	Karen Neubarth
John Ryan	Peg Deutchman

Minutes of the May Board Meeting
were approved as read.

**VICE-
PRESIDENT**

Diane Henkel reported that Irene
Landendorf will assume responsibility
for <u>The Echo</u>.

The Pancake Breakfast, now scheduled
for July 11, will be coordinated
by Gene O'Boyle, Lee Radtke, Sr.,
and Lee Radtke, Jr.

The Family Picnic, scheduled for
August 1, will be handled by
Kay Leavy and Jean Kane.

The Fish Fry, scheduled for September
10, will be supervised by John Ryan.

TREASURER

Karen Neubarth reported:

Dues Collected	$13,270.50
Checking Account	$16,524.70
Savings Account	$26,696.40

LAKE

The Board agreed to increase the
liability insurance from $100,000
to $300,000.

Community residents will be notified
when lake weed treatment will occur.
It is recommended that no swimming

occur for 24 hours after spraying and that any fish caught up to 72 hours after spraying not be eaten.

ROADS AND SANITATION

The problem of unkept property was discussed and is of great concern to the board of directors. It was decided that the following action will be pursued:

   a. Inquiry with Health Department as to action available to the Community and the Board.
   b. Formal protest to be registered by means of a letter to the homeowner.
   c. Opportunity provided for corrective response.
   d. Consideration given to filing civil suit.

Howard Vasey reported on the meeting held by residents of Lone Tree Lane with the County Commissioner. Culverts have been installed which should eliminate the flooding.

The file on easements and pathways to the lake was turned over to Howard Vasey. The next action will be discussions held with persons whose property is involved.

PARK

Cleanup of Community Center, park, and beach will occur June 12.

The original landscaping plan will be completed before any new action is undertaken.

NEW BUSINESS

1. Soliciting. Concerned residents have contacted some board members about increasing numbers of door-to-door salesmen. "No Soliciting" signs will be posted at entrances to the subdivisions.

2. Karen Neubarth reminded board members that all expenses must be approved by the president and that the treasurer should be advised in advance of any major expenditures.

The next board meeting will be July 13.

The meeting was adjourned at 10:10 p.m.

Example 7

COMMUNICATIONS DEPARTMENT

Activity Report

Date: March 1, **19xx**

In Attendance: Editorial
Graphics
Production

Job:	Description:	In:	Out:	DUE:
1205 - Staff Handbook	Manual	1-17		1-4
Status/Comments: In collating 3-3. Due for review 3-9.				
1742 - Business cards	Engraved cards	11-11		11-30
Replacement cards ordered for five executives				
1808 - Business Plan	Plastics Division Plan	11-23		ASAP
Plan received late; division must submit to HQ next week				
1833 - Your Insurance	Employee Booklet	12-7		2-15
Final corrected typeset to editorial 3-4; due in art 3-4				
1839 - Annual Report	Report to Shareholders	12-7		3-30
Photo session scheduled 12-15.				
1883 - Employee Report	Company magazine	12-16		4-1
Photos completed 3-3; will publish on time				
1887 - Productivity	Speech	2-1		4-1
First draft completed - routed for approval				
1905 - Manufacturing	Safety slide presentation	1-1		4-1
Script approved; photography half finished				
1911 - Proposal cover	Standard proposal cover	2-15		3-2
Sales department needs for presentation next week				
1947 - Capabilities	Brochure	3-1		5-1
Redesign and rewrite previous version				
1950 - Shareholder letter	Letter from Chairman	3-1		3-2
Edit and word process letter				

Example 8

To: Albert Williams   Date: May 1, 19xx

From: Janet Wright

Subject: Meeting Room Setup

DATE_June 3, 19xx____   ROOM_Grand Ballroom____

TIME_1:00-5:30 p.m.____   CONTACT_Janet Wright____

FUNCTION____Scientific Sessions and Business Meeting____

ROOM SKETCH & SETUP   REQUIREMENTS

Schoolroom (250) Center Aisle   Platform
                                       Head table with 3
                                         chairs
```
┌───────────────────────────┐         2 Podiums with
│  ┌─────────────────────┐  │           mic & light
│  │       Platform      │  │         2 Lavaliere or
│  │Podium         Podium│  │           lapel mics
│  │     Head Table      │  │         Screen
│  └─────────────────────┘  │         Blackboard/Chalk/
│                           │           Eraser
│                           │         Ash trays on left
│  xxxxxxxx    xxxxxxxxx    │           side only for
│                           │           smoking section
│                           │         Smoking Section
│  xxxxxxxx    xxxxxxxxx    │           sign
│                           │         Water/Ice/Glasses
│                           │
│  xxxxxxxx    xxxxxxxxx    │
│                           │
│    etc.        etc.       │
└───────────────────────────┘
```

Example 9

June 5, 19xx

To: All Catalog Holders

From: F. E. Kennedy

Subject: Hydraulic Cooling on Injection Molding
           Machines

Based on field feedback, we are changing our guidelines for hydraulic cooling for two Molding
Machines Models 300M26 and 125M-8. Each machine
is equipped with a 50-horsepower and 20-horsepower
hydraulic unit. Based on actual field weighed
water tests, we find the actual heat input to be
50 percent greater.

The extra heat input is due to the duty cycle on
the high pressure hydraulic pump. We are recommending .15 tons per one horsepower for hydraulic
cooling.

Example 10

To: Executive Staff   Date: March 17, 19xx

From: Regional Administrator

Subject: Sexual Harassment

This memorandum outlines the Office of Personnel
Management's policy statement on sexual harassment
which is applicable to each federal agency and
department. The policy statement includes the
specific definition of sexual harassment that
should be utilized in addressing this issue.

I am recommending that each of you take a leadership role by making each employee aware of OPM's
policy statement, emphasizing this policy as a
part of new employee orientation covering code of

conduct, and making employees aware of the avenues
for seeking redress and the actions that will be
taken against employees violating the policy.

POLICY STATEMENT AND DEFINITION
ON SEXUAL HARASSMENT

Federal employees have a grave responsibility under
the federal code of conduct and ethics for maintaining high standards of honesty, integrity,
impartiality, and conduct to assure proper performance of the government's business and the
maintenance of confidence of the American people.
Any employee conduct that violates this code cannot
be condoned.

Sexual harassment is a form of employee misconduct
that undermines the integrity of the employment
relationship. All employees must be allowed to
work in an environment free from unsolicited and
unwelcome sexual overtures. Sexual harassment
debilitates morale and interferes in the work
productivity of its victims and coworkers.

Sexual harassment is a prohibited personnel practice
when it results in discrimination for or against an
employee on the basis of conduct not related to
performance, such as the taking or refusal to take
a personnel action, including promotion of employees
who submit to sexual advances or refusal to promote
employees who resist or protest sexual overtures.

Specifically, sexual harassment is deliberate or
repeated unsolicited verbal comments, gestures, or
physical contact of a sexual nature that are unwelcome.

Within the federal government a supervisor who uses
implicit or explicit coercive sexual behavior to
control, influence, or affect the career, salary, or
job of an employee is engaging in sexual harassment.
Similarly, an employee of an agency who behaves in
this manner in the process of conducting agency
business is engaging in sexual harassment.

Finally, any employee who participates in deliberate
or repeated unsolicited verbal comments, gestures,
or physical contact of a sexual nature that are
unwelcome and interfere with work productivity is
also engaging in sexual harassment.

It is the policy of the Office of Personnel Management (OPM) that sexual harassment is unacceptable conduct in the workplace and will not be condoned. Personnel management within the federal sector shall be implemented free from prohibited personnel practices and consistent with merit system principles, as outlined in the provisions of the Civil Service Reform Act of 1978. All federal employees should avoid conduct that undermines these merit principles. At the same time, it is not the intent of OPM to regulate the social interaction of relationships freely entered into by federal employees.

Example 11

To: Publisher

From: Editor

Subject: Analysis of lateness and consequent extra charges in the January issue.

The purpose of this memo is not to blame any individual or department but, rather, to show areas of weakness that can be addressed and strengthened through cooperative effort.

Problem: The publisher's lateness with his message. This page closed one hour before the final deadline due to lateness and corrections that had to be squeezed in while other, much more complicated corrections were being handled.

Solution: If the publisher insists on a brownline close for this page for reasons of timeliness of content, then he should, in good faith to the demands of deadlines placed on all other writers, provide a fallback column in the event that a planned column does not work--as was the case in this issue.

Problem: The editor's holdup of boards in production because he is in a meeting or otherwise engaged.

Solution: The editor will schedule his time so as to allow no meetings to interfere with a smooth flow of boards across his desk. If he is in a meeting, the copy editor should call him out of it and get his attention on the boards during this critical period.

<u>Problem</u>:   Remakes in keylined boards.

<u>Solution</u>:   The editor, articles editor, and associate editor will review all boards in rough pasteup form and make any changes <u>before</u> they go to the keyline department. Only remakes tolerated on keylined boards will be for typos uncaught by typesetting or corrections called for and not made or for changes in space due to alterations in pacing, ad size changes, etc.

<u>Problem</u>:   Changes in brownline proofs.

<u>Solution</u>:   All of the above, plus more organized work flow and attention to deadlines from publisher's office down to the last set of eyes on a board.

Thank you for your cooperation.

17

Interoffice Letters

"The test of a good letter is a very simple one. If one seems to hear the person talking, it is a good letter."

Christopher Benson

Much advice has been given about letter writing, and scores of books have been written on the subject. This chapter deals only with the writing of interoffice letters. If you would like additional general information about letters, refer to the bibliography for some good references on the subject.

One of the first pieces of advice many letter-writing gurus give is: "Write the way you talk." Don't take that advice too literally. Most of us do not speak all that well. If you don't believe it, try tape recording a meeting sometime, transcribe it later, and read what you and the others said. My experience has been that it will take some serious editing to get it into a form that makes sense.

The point the experts are making, I believe, is that most business letters are stuffy. It may be our business heritage, or it may be that because the subject we are writing about is serious, we are serious too.

I am not suggesting that you should be as casual and conversational in business letters as you are in personal correspondence, but neither should your writing style be stilted and unnatural. Put your message in plain, simple language and say what you have to say.

You are competing for the reader's attention just like the

hundreds of others who try to sell the same reader something every day. Most people are simply too busy to try to sift through vague, uncertain messages to try to figure out what you are *not* telling them.

Sharpen your message so that there is no chance that it can be misinterpreted. Do this by deciding in advance exactly what you want the reader to understand when he finishes the letter. Make a list of the points you want to cover and shape the letter around those key points.

Don't try to cover too many things in the same letter. All your points should relate to a single topic. If you have several subjects to cover with the same reader, write separate letters for each major topic. Remember that your reader may circulate the letters to others for comments or handling, and when you try to cover too much, not only do you risk losing the reader's attention, but you also make it more difficult to respond.

Take a look at some of the so-called "junk mail" you receive. If you analyze it carefully, you will find that it is often some of the best letter writing you will ever receive. Every word, every comma is directed toward the end result of selling you something. And there is almost always only one central theme or message.

Direct mail copywriters learned long ago that we readers have a short attention span. If the message is too confusing or complicated, we exercise our supreme freedom and toss the letter into the garbage. Even if your reader is very interested in your message, you have to make it easy to read and respond if you hope to get any action.

When should you write an interoffice letter instead of a memorandum? It depends. As in any business writing consideration, you have to make the decision based on your situation, your company's customs and policies, the personalities of the people to whom you are writing, and any number of other things. There are, however, some guidelines based mostly on tradition and preferences.

If the situation you are writing about seems to be formal enough to demand more than a memo, if you are responding to a letter from someone in the company, or if others outside the company are getting a copy of the correspondence, you may prefer to send a letter. Additionally, if you are writing to your employees or coworkers at home, it is customary to write a letter instead of a memo.

The types of letters that might most often be used in interoffice situations would include:

- confirming letters;
- affirmative letters;
- negative letters;
- contingency letters;
- solicitation letters;
- follow-up letters;
- victory letters;
- defeat letters; and
- problem letters.

Let's take a look at each type and how they might be constructed in an ideal situation.

Confirming Letters

A confirming letter would most likely be used in situations in which two or more units of the same company are corresponding and copies are being sent to others outside the company. A more common approach would be to write to the outsider and send a copy to the fellow employee, but there are special situations that call for special solutions.

Here is an actual example that called for a special solution. Conflicting opinions existed between two departments of the same firm, and an outside consultant who assisted both groups on occasion was attempting to set a meeting to resolve the dispute. Both departments agreed that it was a good idea to meet, and one confirmed the meeting to the other. Copies were sent to the consultant and others in the company. The following is the text of that letter.

Dear Gene:

At various times in the past we have talked about the possibility of developing an audiovisual program about our company to be presented at our annual shareholders' meeting. I understand your reservations about such a presentation in view of our recent earnings; however, there are some circumstances that we should consider.

- Investor relations. Our earnings and profits
  are public knowledge. Ducking the issue is
  no guarantee that we won't address it in the
  question-and-answer session.

- Media relations. We will, no doubt, have a
  representative or two from the business press
  in attendance. They would, in effect, be a
  captive audience for telling our story in a
  favorable way.

Let's talk about these considerations at our
meeting.

For your assistance, I am enclosing a summary
of the questions that were raised at the last
shareholders' meeting and the meeting evaluations
from our own people. Please take a moment to review this information prior to the meeting.

I have reserved the conference room on your
floor from 9:00 a.m. until noon on December 2. I
will look forward to seeing you then.

If, in the meantime, you need additional
information, please give me a call.

                    Sincerely,

                    William A. Provost

cc: P. K. Hall

Enclosures

Affirmative Letters

These letters are the easiest to write. If the news is good, it is hard to tell it in a manner that will offend the reader. It is possible, however, to take advantage of a positive situation and get a little more mileage out of your efforts.

Tell your reader the good news right away, tell him why you responded favorably, and congratulate him on his success. After all, next time you may have to respond negatively, and it will be easier then if you can point to a previous positive response. Make sure he remembers the style and finesse with which you granted an earlier request.

Here's an example.

Dear Fred:

   I am pleased to inform you that your article about your customer's printing plant has been accepted for publication in the fall issue of our company publication.

   I think our readers will find the article interesting and informative. I don't know if you are aware of the makeup of our readership, but in addition to our own 10,000-plus employees, we enjoy a circulation of more than 100,000 customers, paper merchants, and other business associates.

   In order to recognize your achievement properly, by copy of this letter, I am asking our public relations agency to prepare a publicity release for distribution to your hometown news media when the article is published. Please send your biographical sketch and a recent black-and-white glossy photo to:

> Michael Murphy
> Vice-President
> Murphy, Miller & Associates
> 2121 First Street
> Anywhere, U.S.A. 00001

If you do not wish to have a publicity release prepared, no action is necessary. The receipt of your photo and biography triggers the release preparation.

Congratulations on this achievement.

Sincerely yours,

I. M. Wordsmith
Editor-in-Chief

cc: Michael Murphy

Negative Letters

Saying no to anyone is difficult, whether it is done in a memo, in a letter, or in person. The larger the stakes are, the more difficult it is to deny the request. Most of us would much prefer to respond in the affirmative, yet it is a fact of life that we can't always say yes.

Before you begin writing a letter that tells your reader that you can't comply with the request, think about how you would respond in a similar situation. Put yourself in the reader's place. How would you feel? How would you like to be told? Think about the times you have had the same or similar experiences.

As in writing memos giving bad news, the best way to approach the problem is head-on. Tell the reader right away that the request was denied or that the news is bad. Then tell him why. If we can learn something from an unsuccessful attempt, most of us can accept a negative response more easily.

If the decision is not negotiable, however, don't make your

response so warm and cordial that you encourage everyone whose request you deny to call you to talk about it. Be firm and direct.

The following is an example of a negative response.

Dear Lee:

I am sorry to inform you that we will be unable to grant your request for a transfer to our San Francisco office.

At the present time we have a full complement of account representatives and several other transfer requests ahead of yours. As you know, our office is rather small, and we do not often have openings that suit your background and experience. When we do, we attempt to extend the opportunity to our own employees first.

I would suggest that you contact the Corporate Director of Human Resources to review any other openings in the company that might fit your career goals. Your past achievements indicate you would be an asset to any office, and we will certainly keep your request on file in the event our situation changes.

I wish you every success in your other endeavors.

Sincerely yours,

Douglas M. Cunningham
General Manager

Contingency Letters

There are few absolutes in life and fewer yet in business. It seems that almost everything is based on a contingency. Perhaps the request can be granted if the circumstances are right or if more information is provided.

In this event the tone of the letter should be somewhere between the firm but fair denial letter and the cordial and congratulatory affirmative letter. You not only want to leave your reader an opening to discuss it; you also want to encourage further discussion.

Here is an example of a contingency letter.

Dear Mr. Adler:

Our group health insurance carrier has reviewed your claim in connection with surgery performed by Dr. Hamilton Johnston on March 18, 19xx. The company has approved a maximum payment of $750.

Surgical benefits are determined based on the "reasonable and customary" fee for the operation you underwent. It is a historical average of what surgeons in this area charge for such a surgical procedure and, as such, is more of a statistical figure than a judgmental one.

Our insurance company recognizes, of course, that there are sometimes extenuating circumstances. Unless the physician indicates unusual or non-standard conditions on the claim form, however, the standard fee is paid.

If the physician certifies that unusual conditions did exist, and describes them, the insurance

```
company will reconsider the claim.  I would suggest

that you discuss this with Dr. Johnston, and if you

would like to pursue this avenue, please get in

touch with me.  I would be pleased to advise you

of the procedure.

                    Sincerely yours,

                    Mary Jane Peoples
                    Personnel Manager
```

Solicitation Letters

If you are assigned the task of writing a solicitation letter, you have a difficult assignment, indeed. We all receive them, and most of us have limited funds to contribute to the cause, however worthwhile it may be.

In addition, the competition is keen. Not only do your fellow employees receive requests from many civic, business, and political organizations; they are solicited by other coworkers, as well.

By virtue of the fact that you both work for the same company, you do have an advantage that outsiders don't. You know that your letter will be opened if it is from the company you both work for, and if you write it well, it may be read. If you are persuasive, the response may be favorable.

Capitalize on your strengths and use your company affiliation to an advantage. Appeal to your readers' community spirit; sell them on the reasons for contributing. (*Note:* You should check your company's policy for soliciting contributions from employees. Since employees support a wide range of causes, many firms have strict guidelines for soliciting contributions from company personnel.)

Here is an example of a solicitation letter.

```
Dear Janet/Ms. Krebbs (depending on how well you
                       know the recipient):

    I am writing you at home for two reasons:

        ● First, I wanted to reach you at a
```

time when you are away from the
activity in the office.

- Second, what I am writing about reflects a personal rather than professional commitment.

What I am speaking of is the annual crusade
to raise funds for those in our community who need
our help. I know this is only one of many letters
you receive asking for contributions, but before
you toss this one into the garbage, I ask you to review the assistance made possible by contributors
to last year's crusade:

1. subsidies to allow continued
   operation of our senior citizens'
   bus service;

2. financial assistance to more than
   200 deserving college students;

3. Christmas toys for more than 500
   children who might not have otherwise received a visit from Santa; and

4. food and clothing for hundreds of
   families who need help just to
   maintain a minimum standard of
   living.

The list goes on, but I think you get the idea.
Without our help the crusade would be unable to help

so many with services that are desperately needed.

This is our opportunity to give something back
to the community that has given so much to us
collectively as a corporation doing business here
and as individuals who prosper personally based on
our firm's success.

As chairman of this year's crusade, it is my
pleasant responsibility to invite you to join the
hundreds of others in our company who have so
generously supported the crusade for every one of
the fifty years Acme Corporation has been head-
quartered in this city.

Please take a few minutes to review the
enclosed brochure, which describes, better than I
ever could, the assistance the crusade continues
to give. If, after reading it, you agree with me
that it is a worthwhile cause that deserves your
support, you may make your contribution simply
by completing and returning the enclosed postage-
paid reply postcard authorizing a payroll deduction.

Thank you for your consideration.

Sincerely,

Ed Weiss

Enclosures

P.S. Your contribution is tax deductible. At the
end of the year the Accounting Department will

provide you with written documentation of your

contribution that you may attach to your income

tax return.

Follow-Up Letters

With the blizzard of paperwork most office workers deal with every day, it is easy for one piece to get lost in the shuffle. If you have not received a response to an earlier letter, if the situation has changed since your last letter, or if you believe that enough time has passed to send a second request, you may want to follow up with another letter on the same topic.

Let's assume several months have passed since you received the negative response in the earlier transfer example and that the situation has changed. You have been offered a transfer to the Monterey, California, office, but before making a final decision you would like to check San Francisco once more. Your follow-up letter might be written like this:

Dear Mr. Cunningham:

A few months ago I wrote to you asking you to

consider me for a transfer to the San Francisco

office.

Since then several things have happened that

may interest you. Some of the more noteworthy are:

- My sales are up 30 percent over last

  year, and well ahead of plan.

- I have opened several new accounts and

  more than doubled sales to four of my

  current customers.

- I placed first in sales in my region

  for the last calendar year and was well

ahead of the second place winner.

- At the end of the year I was promoted
  to senior account representative.

I have recently been offered a transfer to
the Monterey office, but San Francisco is still my
first choice. I am enclosing a copy of an up-to-
date resume that details my recent achievements. I
would appreciate your reviewing it to determine
whether conditions have changed sufficiently for
you to reconsider my request to transfer to the
San Francisco office.

I will telephone you in a few days to discuss
your interest. Such a move, I am convinced, would
be mutually profitable.

Sincerely yours,

Lee Roberts

Victory Letters

As the old saying goes, one should be magnanimous in victory
and gracious in defeat. When you enjoy a successful venture,
waste no time in reassuring the decision makers that they made
the right decision and be kind to the losers.

Let's assume that you resolved the insurance dispute from the
contingency example in your favor. Follow up with a letter to the
personnel manager expressing appreciation for assistance rendered and mend some fences along the way.

Here is an example.

Dear Ms. Peoples:

Thank you for your assistance in resolving my

disputed claim with our group insurance carrier.

I am pleased to report that the full amount of the claim will be paid.

Following denial of the claim the second time (after additional information was provided), I appealed the decision to the Peer Review Board. The board met last week and decided in my favor.

I understand the importance of close monitoring of health insurance claims and that both you and the companies that underwrite our insurance coverage must be very cautious about unusual claims. I hope the problems that resulted from my pursuit of this matter did not unduly inconvenience either you or the insurance company.

Thank you for your advice and assistance.

Sincerely,

B. A. Adler
Production Supervisor

cc: A.P. Ratoc
    Group Insurance Company

Defeat Letters

Now for the gracious loser. Nobody likes to lose, but in a competitive situation there is room for only one winner. For losers there is more opportunity. Losing letters should be easier to write, since we statistically have more chances to write them. Unfortunately, it doesn't work that way. Losing a proposal or being turned down for a promotion causes emotions to get in the way of objectivity.

Let's assume that a big project for which you were sure of winning approval was rejected. Your gracious losing letter might be written as follows.

Dear Bill:

    Thank you for your letter advising me that my project was not approved at the last board meeting.

    Naturally, I'm disappointed, but I would like to learn as much as I can about the board's reasoning so that the next time I submit a proposal it will have a better chance of success.

    I plan to be in Atlanta near the end of the month and would like to discuss this with you. I won't take much of your time, and your advice and assistance will help me direct future proposals toward areas that are more in keeping with the board's goals and objectives.

    I will telephone you next week to check your availability during my visit.

                  Cordially,

                  Mitchell Owings
                  Director of Manufacturing

Problem Letters

Until now it's been easy. You have had a few rough spots and some fairly difficult letter-writing assignments, but how do you handle those really tough problems?

The answer is the same in any type of writing. Think about your readers, be sensitive to their needs, and be straightforward and direct in your writing.

One of the most difficult situations in any line of business is to tell someone that he is terminated. Usually, such problems would be handled in person by the employee's supervisor, but what happens if it's a massive layoff?

Even if you hold a meeting to tell all the employees at once, you should follow up in writing to tell the recipients what you are doing to help them and what alternatives, if any, exist.

Here is an example of a problem letter.

Dear Mr. Meeks:

It is with profound regret that I must inform you that the Columbia, South Carolina, plant will be closed at the end of the month.

As I'm sure you know, our textile business has declined substantially during recent years, and continuing losses have forced us to get out of the business. We have reached an agreement to sell the Textile Division, but the new owners have other more modern facilities elsewhere that will manufacture products now being made in Columbia.

To assist you in relocation, the company will establish an outplacement office in Columbia. Qualified applicants will be considered for any openings throughout the company, and we will attempt to place Columbia employees in other companies in the area.

You will receive four weeks severance and additional pay at your standard rate for accrued vacation time. Your insurance coverage will remain in force for one month after your final paycheck, and you may convert it to private coverage if you

wish.   Conversion information will be sent to you
with your final paycheck.

Thank you for your service to the company and
good luck with your relocation efforts.

Very truly yours,

Albert Kindness,
President

LETTER FORMATS

Many companies have policies and procedures manuals dealing
with correspondence and secretarial manuals describing approved
formats. If you have no established policies, use one of the
following examples as a guide.

S. A. CYPERT

23957 N. LAKEWOOD DRIVE
LAKE ZURICH, ILLINOIS 60047
312-438-3498

Date (12 spaces from top of page, 4 to 8 spaces
      from bottom of letterhead.)

(5 spaces)

Mr./Mrs./Ms. Last Name
Title
Company
Address
City, State, Zip
(2 spaces)
Dear Mr./Mrs./Ms. Last Name: (First name if you know
    the person well)
(2 spaces)
I am writing to express what I believe is a real need
in our company: consistency in written communications.
(2 spaces)
Since we have no uniform correspondence policy, one

could place any half-dozen letters from our employees
side by side and never know they came from the same
company, save for the common letterhead. If you
placed letters from our various operating divisions
alongside each other, you would really be uncertain
where they came from, since each uses its own corporate
identification.
(2 spaces)
I suggest that we engage an outside firm that specialize
in such identity crises to review our antiquated
correspondence manual and develop some modern, workable
guidelines that we can all follow. Presenting the
company in a consistent, uniform manner would enhance
our recognition with our customers, the general public,
and our employees.
(2 spaces)
I would be pleased to chair such a committee and will
phone you next week to discuss this idea with you.
(2 spaces)
Sincerely yours/Sincerely/Very truly yours/Cordially,
(4 spaces)

Your Name,
Your Title
(2 spaces)

cc: (if any)
Enclosures

S. A. Cypert

23957 N. LAKEWOOD DRIVE
LAKE ZURICH, ILLINOIS 60047
312-438-3498

                        Date (12 spaces from top of
                             page, 4 to 8 spaces from
                             bottom of letterhead.)

(5 spaces)

Mr./Mrs./Ms. Last Name
Title
Company
Address
City, State, Zip
(2 spaces)
Dear Mr./Mrs./Ms. Last Name: (First name if you
   know the person well)
(2 spaces)
     I am writing to express what I believe is a real
need in our company: consistency in written
communications.
(2 spaces)
     Since we have no uniform correspondence policy,
one could place any half-dozen letters from our employees
side by side and never know they came from the same
company, save for the common letterhead. If you placed
letters from our various operating divisions alongside
each other, you would really be uncertain where they
came from, since each uses its own corporate
identification.
(2 spaces)
     I suggest that we engage an outside firm that
specializes in such identity crises to review our
antiquated correspondence manual and develop some
modern, workable guidelines that we can all follow.
Presenting the company in a consistent, uniform manner
would enhance our recognition with our customers, the
general public, and our employees.
(2 spaces)
     I would be pleased to chair such a committee and

will phone you next week to discuss this idea with you.
(2 spaces)

                        Sincerely yours/Sincerely/
                        Very truly yours/Cordially,
                        (4 spaces)

                        Your Name
                        Your Title

(2 spaces)
cc: (if any)
Enclosures

18

A Word about Grammar

"A language is something infinitely greater than grammar and philology. It is the poetic testament of the genius of a race and a culture, and the living embodiment of the thoughts and fancies that have moulded them."

Jawaharlal Nehru

Not infrequently in discussions with authors of reports, proposals, and other important documents issued by companies I am asked: "Is the correct use of grammar really all that important?" And the answer is: "To some readers it is not important at all."

The difficulty lies in the fact that we don't usually know which of our readers attach very little importance to precision in language and which insist on it. It's like the English soap manufacturer William Lever's comment on advertising: "Half the money I spend on advertising is wasted; the trouble is, I don't know which half."

And so it is with correctness. Your efforts may be wasted on half your audience, but the difficulty is in determining which half.

If you are attempting to explain a difficult or complex concept in a report, or if you are trying to sell management on funding a project, precise language, correctly used, may not always guarantee success but can only help your efforts. Carelessness and incorrect usage, on the other hand, may not guarantee failure but may hinder your chances for success. Proper use of the language is important.

In the past few years I have had the opportunity to talk to many groups about writing skills, and when the topic of grammar comes up, meeting participants usually groan and roll their eyes in obvious disapproval. Most of us associate grammar rules with unpleasant experiences in school, when many of us tried unsuccessfully to understand the rules.

The English language is, in fact, often vague and subject to interpretation. Professional writers and editors often disagree about the fine points of the language, and if you locked two grammarians in the same room and told them they couldn't come out until they agreed on everything about the use of the language, you would probably have to slide food and books under the door forever. They would never come out.

There is a payoff, however, for all those difficult days spent in language classes in the course of your education. You probably know more about correct usage than you think you do. You may not remember exactly why you shouldn't end a sentence in formal writing with a preposition, but you know it doesn't look right and sound right.

The best way I know to tap that secret knowledge you already have when something doesn't appear quite right is to look it up. It is also a good idea to read aloud difficult passages or those about which you are uncertain. Your mind has a way of working with greater intensity when you use both your visual and auditory senses, and reading it aloud also forces you to slow down, which further heightens your concentration.

In business writing the proof is in the success of the project. It doesn't matter how you managed to write it correctly, only that you did. Once you are past the formal education process you are not expected to remember all those vague and confusing rules. All you have to know is where to find them.

REFERENCE BOOKS

The following is a list of references that you will find helpful in assuring the accuracy of your work. Publication dates are omitted due to frequent revisions. For other references related to specific areas of writing (e.g., proposals and reports), please refer to the bibliography.

Dictionaries

- *The American Heritage Dictionary of the English Language.* Boston: Houghton Mifflin Company.
- *Funk & Wagnalls New Practical Standard Dictionary.* New York: Funk & Wagnalls Company.
- *The Random House Dictionary of the English Language.* New York: Random House.
- *Webster's Eighth New Collegiate Dictionary.* Springfield, MA: G&C Merriam Co.
- *Webster's Third New International Dictionary.* Springfield, MA: G&C Merriam Co.

Language and Grammar Aids

- Hodges, John C., and Whitten, Mary E. *Harbrace College Handbook:* New York/Chicago/San Francisco/Atlanta: Harcourt Brace Jovanovich, Inc.
- Bernstein, Theodore M. *The Careful Writer: A Guide to English Usage.* New York: Atheneum.
- Flesch, Rudolph. *The Art of Readable Writing.* New York: Harper and Row.
- Gunning, Robert. *The Technique of Clear Writing.* New York: McGraw-Hill Book Company.
- Strunk, William Jr., and White, E. B. *The Elements of Style.* New York: Macmillan.
- Venolia, Janet G. *Write Right!* Woodland Hills, CA: Periwinkle Press.

Word Guides

- *Roget's Pocket Thesaurus.* New York: Pocket Books, Inc. Division of Simon & Schuster.
- *Roget's International Thesaurus of English Words and Phrases.* New York: Thomas Y. Crowell Company.
- *The Merriam-Webster Pocket Dictionary of Synonyms.* New York: Pocket Books, Inc. Division of Simon & Schuster.
- *Webster's New Dictionary of Synonyms.* Springfield: MA: G&C Merriam Co.

Style Guides

- *A Manual of Style*. Chicago: The University of Chicago Press.
- *Style Manual*. Washington, DC: United States Government Printing Office.
- *Words into Type*. Englewood Cliffs, NJ: Prentice-Hall, Inc.

COMMON MISTAKES AND HOW TO AVOID THEM

For some reason most writers have blind spots about various uses of words, make the same grammatical mistakes, or misspell the same words. If you review your own work, you will probably find that you tend to make the same errors until someone points them out to you or until you accidentally discover them in checking a reference for some other purpose. Even after we discover our grammatical mistakes it is very often difficult to correct them.

Other mistakes in writing more properly fall into the area of judgment. Writing is a series of choices—of words, phrases, ideas, styles, and many more other elements that go into the construction of a good piece of writing. Judgmental mistakes may be even more difficult to correct than grammatical ones.

The following list includes common mistakes that I (and, no doubt, legions of other business writers and editors) have run across in the course of a career in communications. Suggestions for improvement are included in each category. Some material from Chapter 2 has been included in this alphabetical listing for easy reference.

Active Form

Use a personal and active structure in your writing so your reader will feel that you are one actual person writing to another actual person.

Active: It is my fervent hope that you read this book and profit from it.

Passive: It is fervently hoped that this book is read by you and that it is proven to be profitable.

The exception, where the passive construction might be more desirable, would be in instances in which the receiver of the action is more important than the doer or in establishing objectivity in report writing.

Agreement

The subject must agree with the verb in number; pronouns must agree with their antecedents. Singular subjects take singular verbs; plural subjects take plural verbs.

> *Examples:* A report *writer is* seldom as thorough as *he* should be. (singular)
> Report *writers are* seldom as thorough as *they* should be. (plural)

Subjects joined by *and* (compound subjects) usually require a plural verb.

> *Example:* A report *writer and an editor* working as a team *are* usually more thorough than either individual is when working alone.

The difficulty in making certain that subjects agree with verbs arises when they are separated by other phrases. Break the sentence down to its basic parts to identify subjects and verbs.

Singular subjects joined by *or, neither,* or *either* usually take a singular verb.

> *Example: Neither* the writer of the report nor its editor *was* present at the initial strategy meeting.

Completeness

This topic falls into both the judgmental and grammatical categories.

In the area of judgment, written thoughts and ideas should be complete. Never assume your reader will understand certain parts and that other portions need more explanation. If only one element of a report or proposal is misunderstood by the reader, it could very well alter your chances of success.

In construction, use complete sentences. You may say it is common knowledge that we should use complete sentences. It is; but very often, incomplete sentences creep in, partially, I suspect, because we edit our portions and forget to check for completeness. Also, we talk in incomplete sentences at times, and we have become accustomed to incomplete sentences in advertising and broadcast news reports.

Make sure your sentences have a subject and a verb.

Consistency

Be consistent in your use of acronyms and abbreviations. If you use one acronym in one place and a different one later, you jar your reader. Keeping usage consistent keeps the text flowing smoothly. It is customary to put an abbreviation or acronym in parentheses immediately after it appears in its unabridged form the first time. The abbreviated version may then be used as a substitute for the full term.

It is also advisable to be consistent in your style of presentation. Don't be formal in one portion of the document and chatty in other sections. Follow the same style throughout.

If different people write portions of a long document, edit it to make sure it is consistent.

Misplaced Modifiers

It is a good idea to keep modifiers close to the words they modify in order to avoid confusion and awkward constructions. In some instances having modifiers in the wrong place changes the meaning of the sentences; in every instance the construction is not as good as it should be.

Example: I saw an old man walking a dog smoking a pipe.

The question becomes: Who was smoking the pipe, the man or the dog? Keeping the phrase *smoking a pipe* next to the word *man,* the word it is intended to modify, clarifies the sentence.

Dangling modifiers are a type of misuse of modifiers. They

occur when the word or phrase that should be modified is left out. These will sometimes fool you because they appear to be correct at first. It is only after you try to locate the parts of the sentence that it becomes apparent something is missing.

> *Example:* After attending the strategy session, writing the proposal was easy.

In this example, there is no subject. It should read: After I attended the strategy session, writing the proposal was easy.

Parallel Construction

Thoughts should be parallel, and sentence constructions should be parallel. The use of parallel construction is an aid to understanding. The reader can relate ideas and concepts to follow your line of reasoning, but you should make certain that the ideas are related. Do not use a parallel construction for unrelated thoughts.

Wrong: Advertising types cannot understand accountants, who are interested in balancing the books and the columns must foot.
Better: Advertising types cannot understand accountants who are interested in making sure the books balance and the columns foot.

To avoid misunderstandings you can repeat the infinitive, the preposition, or the introductory word.

> *Example:* After the report is finished we will proofread it to check for spelling errors, to ensure precision in language, and to make sure punctuation is correct.

If you use bullet points or lists, make sure the items used in the bullets form a complete thought when read with the introductory phrase and that they are parallel.

Wrong: The purpose of this proposal is to provide information about:
- our technical staff
- performing other similar projects; and
- our qualifications.

Better: The purpose of this proposal is to provide information about our:
- technical staff;
- experience in similar projects; and
- qualifications.

Use parallel construction and ideas to enhance the rhythm and flow of ideas.

Example: "It is easy in the world to live after the world's opinion—it is easy in solitude to live after your own; but the great man is he who, in the midst of the world, keeps with perfect sweetness the independence of solitude."   —Ralph Waldo Emerson

Pomposity

Another obvious point, you say. Your writing should never be pompous. Nevertheless, it is a common affliction in business writing.

The principal offenses I have observed are in those cases in which the writer either talks down to the reader, thereby insulting his intelligence, or talks over his head, thereby confusing him or making him feel inferior. It is not easy to address the reader in descriptive, interesting language that he understands and relates to, and many writers don't bother to try.

If you understand your readers and have done your audience analysis, and if you write in forthright, appropriate language, your reader will appreciate it, and you won't come across as being pompous.

Avoid exaggerated claims. Even if your idea will do splendid things, don't rave about those things. Let the facts speak for themselves. Present the information in such a believable way that the reader reaches his own conclusion—that this is a splendid idea.

Don't use words you are not absolutely sure about, even if you saw them used in the same context. Check them out. Very often, in business writing, information comes from a variety of sources. You may, for example, pick up quotations from published articles, make notes during speeches, and extract information from other interoffice documents. If you are not absolutely sure about the use and context of a word, look it up. The first writer may have misused it.

Sexism

The English language is sexist. It is common, for example, to see writers use the masculine pronoun when the gender is unknown. It is unlikely that *he and she,* or *he/she* will ever replace *he* in that context. It is too unwieldy in spoken usage and too wordy in written usage.

The most viable alternative is to rewrite the offending passages whenever possible to eliminate any reference to sex.

> *Example:* Every recipient of preprinted checks should check them to make sure his name is spelled correctly.
> *Better:* Recipients of preprinted checks should check them to make sure all the information is correct.

There are some situations, however, in which the sentence cannot be written to neutralize the gender without either changing the meaning or making the construction awkward. In such cases many use the masculine form to denote mankind rather than males.

The use of *Ms.* is correct if you are uncertain about a female's marital status. (I know; that in itself is sexist. *Mr.* makes no distinction between married and unmarried men.) I am frequently asked how to treat the use of *Ms.* if you do not know the marital status and do not know if the woman receiving the letter will be offended by its use. My advice is to telephone and find out. If this person is important enough for you to be worrying about the correct salutation, she is important enough for you to find out what is correct.

When you are writing to an organization instead of a specific person, avoid the salutation *Gentlemen:* by using a form similar to the following: *To the Board of Directors:* or *Dear Information Services Manager:*.

Specific Words

Use the right word in its purest form, and don't use technical jargon that is peculiar to one industry or profession. Technical people often become so familiar with the language of their profession and communicate with others in the field in jargon so often that it becomes second nature to them. Remember your audience analysis. Your reader may have no idea of what you are talking about.

Don't use the noun form of a verb when the verb itself is more powerful and will work better. Set priorities; don't prioritize.

Style

Use the appropriate style and tone for the document you are writing. If you are writing an internal audit report detailing misuses of funds and mismanagement of company resources, it certainly won't add anything to your credibility if you write a chatty, informal account of what you found wrong. Conversely, a memo to a close associate need not be formal.

Trust your instincts as to the best style of presentation based on your subject matter and how well you know the recipients.

Use direct language, active and positive constructions, and correct words.

Don't mimic the style of other writers. Go to the files to see what others said, if you wish, but write it in your own words.

Transitions

This one is sometimes difficult to focus on. If you read your composition after you have "let it cool" for a few days and, upon rereading, it seems choppy in construction, you probably need a few bridges between ideas. Lead the reader gently, smoothly through a series of related ideas bridged by transition sentences.

Facilitate the transition by arranging the information in a logical order and link thoughts by their common denominator, such as similar characteristics, or use comparisons to emphasize similarities.

Use phrases like *in addition to, on the other hand, in comparison to, in contrast with,* and the like to make transitions. Typical transition words are *also, additionally, conversely, however, moreover,* and *and so forth.*

Variety

Use variety both in your ideas and in the construction of sentences.

Comparisons of different methods of performing two tasks and using different methods of gathering information are examples of variety in ideas. Such variety not only makes your writing more interesting; it also makes it more believable.

Variety in construction includes alternating short and long sentences to break the monotony and using lists, bullet points, numbers, and dashes to present information in a series.

Verbosity

Eliminate unnecessary words. When you edit what you have written, keep an eye out for unnecessary articles such as *a, an, the* that can be omitted without changing the meaning. Strike out *that* in all but the essential uses. Watch for modifiers that are not really essential to convey the meaning and edit out duplicate or redundant words, phrases, sentences, and paragraphs.

Be especially tough on boilerplate descriptions you extracted from other sources. Cut until there is nothing left but the essence.

Avoid overkill. When you have covered the topic, stop.

PUNCTUATION TIPS

Punctuation tips included in this section deal with most common business usage and are arranged in alphabetical order.

Apostrophe

Use the apostrophe to show possession by:
* Adding an apostrophe and an *s* to nouns not ending in *s*.

   Example: Joe's report

* Adding an apostrophe only to plural nouns that end in *s*.

   Example: boys' coats

- Taking your chances with singular nouns that end in *s*. Here, the experts differ. Some say add both the apostrophe and an *s,* while others say the proper usage is the apostrophe only. Given an option, I prefer the form that uses fewer letters and recommend the addition of the apostrophe only.

  Example: business' cash flow

- Adding an apostrophe and an *s* to show combined possession.

  Example: Joe and Harry's report (They wrote the report together.)

- Adding an apostrophe and an *s* to each to show individual possession.

  Example: Joe's or Harry's report (They each wrote a report.)

Other uses of the apostrophe include:
- To indicate omitted letters in contractions.

  Example: it's, don't

- To indicate plurals of abbreviations or with letters used alone, when the addition of an *s* would be confusing.

  Example: Oakland A's (avoids confusion with the word "As").

Asterisk

Technically, the asterisk may be used to indicate a footnote; however, because it is such a dominant mark, it is usually better to use numbers for footnotes.

Asterisks are sometimes used instead of dashes, numbers, or bullet points in a series.

Colon

Use a colon as follows.
1. To precede a list.

> *Example:* When you go to the store, bring back these
> items: bread, milk, sugar, and salt.

2. To precede a series of bullet points.
3. Before a long formal quotation.

> *Example:* George Washington said: "It is truly our
> policy to steer clear of permanent alliances
> with any portion of the foreign world."

4. After the salutation of a business letter.

> *Example:* Dear Mrs. Jones:

Comma

The comma is tricky. It is the most frequently used of all
punctuation marks and most likely the most misused. In the
following examples the most frequent uses of commas are illustrated and explained. They are listed in alphabetical order.

1. *Appositives.* Nouns placed next to other nouns to provide
   additional information about them or to identify them are
   called *appositives.* They are almost always nonrestrictive
   (words that provide information but are not essential to the
   meaning of the sentence). Use commas to set off nonrestrictive appositives.

   > *Example:* John Thompson, our consultant, joined us
   > for dinner.

2. *Conjunctions.* Use commas before conjunctions—*and, or,
   for, nor, but*—joining independent clauses.

Example: "Age does not depend upon years but upon temperament and health. Some men are born old, and some never grow so."
                                    —Tyron Edwards

Do not use a comma between an independent clause and a dependent clause joined by a conjunction.

Example: "Age is rarely despised but when it is contemptible."   —Samuel Johnson

3. *Consecutive or coordinate adjectives.* Use a comma (instead of the conjunction *and*) to separate adjectives that modify the same word.

Example: The tall, beautiful blonde is my sister.

4. *Contrasting phrases.* Use commas to set off contrasting phrases and clauses.

Example: The high interest rate, not the purchase price, was the principal reason we decided not to buy the building.

5. *Dependent clauses.* When a dependent clause precedes the main clause, it should be separated by a comma.

Example: When he gave us the report, Earl reminded us that our manufacturing expenses are the cause of our losing money.

6. *Direct address.* Use commas to set off a direct address.

Example: As we pointed out earlier, gentlemen, the staffing is insufficient for this project.

7. *Independent clauses.* Use commas before conjunctions separating independent clauses. (See item 2, conjunctions.)

8. *Introductory words, phrases, and clauses.* Use a comma to set off introductory phrases.

Example: In our company, everyone is required to
follow a consistent editorial style.

9. *Numbers and dates.* Use commas to set off complete dates
and between series of numbers where omission would cause
confusion.

Examples: I was born on August 5, 1943, in a farm-
house on the Oklahoma prairie. (com-
plete date)
September 1970 marked our fiftieth anni-
versary. (partial date)
In 1970, 125 million people lived in the
United States. (to avoid confusion)

10. *Omission indicator.* Use the comma to indicate an omission
of a word or phrase.

Example: "The first ingredient in conversation is
truth; the next, good sense; the third,
good humor; and the fourth, wit."
                                    —Sir William Temple

11. *Nonrestrictive clauses and phrases.* Those that are not
essential to the meaning of the sentence should be set off by
commas.

Example: Major reports, which we often issue,
should always include an executive summary.

12. *Restrictive clauses and phrases.* Clauses and phrases that
are essential to the meaning of the sentence are said to be
restrictive and are not set off by commas.

Example: A major report that does not include an
executive summary may not be read.

13. *Parenthetical words and phrases.* Parenthetical elements
are those that are nonrestrictive and often interrupt the

sentence almost as though they were contained in parentheses.

> *Examples:* My mother is a Democrat; my father, on
> the other hand, is a Republican.
> In a report, as in a proposal, planning is
> the secret of success.

14. *Pauses.* Use a comma to indicate a pause that is necessary to avoid confusion.

> *Example:* "Beauty is truth, truth beauty."
> —John Keats

15. *Places.* Use commas to set off certain geographical locations.

> *Example:* I recently returned from visiting our
> Rapid City, South Dakota, offices.

16. *Quotations.* Use commas to set off direct quotations.

> *Example:* "The secret of education," said Ralph
> Waldo Emerson, "lies in respecting the
> pupil."

17. *Series.* Use commas to separate words in a series.

> *Example:* The proposal contained our specifications,
> timetables, reporting relationships, and
> fees.

Dash

Use the dash (two hyphens on a typewriter) when you want more emphasis than commas or parentheses provide.

> *Examples:* "It used to be a good hotel, but that proves
> nothing—I used to be a good boy."
> —Mark Twain
>
> There are many important things—some
> essential—that must be included if the report is
> widely read.

Exclamation Mark

There are very few occasions—if any—when the exclamation mark is used in business writing.

Hyphen

The hyphen is used to join certain combinations of letters, numbers, and words into one unit and as an aid in avoiding confusion or ambiguity.

> *Examples:* three-fourths
> T-square
> state-of-the-art
> short- and long-term investments

Hyphens are also used to indicate word divisions at the right-hand margin. Words should always be divided between syllables; if you are uncertain about where a word should break, check your dictionary.

Numbers

Usually, newspaper editors spell out numbers under ten; book editors spell out numbers under 100. Arabic designations are used for larger numbers, except when a sentence begins with a number.

If you use larger numbers, substitute words for zeros whenever possible.

> *Examples:* There were nine of us on the committee.
> Twenty people applied for the position.
> The total cost was $1.5 million.

Parentheses

Parentheses may be used in a sentence in place of commas or dashes to set off parenthetical elements.

> *Example:* We instructed the salesmen (although they had been told before) to complete the call report summaries.

Parentheses are also used to set off numbers in the text.

Example: There are four items to be considered: (1) costs, (2) service, (3) quality, and (4) delivery.

Punctuation when using parentheses is as follows.
• Enclose punctuation in the parentheses if they contain a complete thought.

Example: We instructed the salesmen to complete the call report summaries. (We had told them before.)

• Put the punctuation outside the parentheses if the parenthetical element does not express a complete thought.

Examples: When we instructed the salesmen to fill out call reports (as we had before), they promised to do so.
We instructed the salesmen to complete the call report summaries (as we had before).

Period

Use a period to end declarative sentences and after abbreviations.

Examples: We received our instructions from headquarters.
Mr., Mrs., Ms., Ph.D.

Question Mark

A question mark appears at the end of a direct question but not an indirect one.

Examples: She asked: "Are we working for the plaintiff or the defendant?" (direct)
She asked if we are working for the plaintiff or the defendant. (indirect)

Quotation Mark

Direct quotations, words used in an unusual way, and titles of articles or other portions of a larger work, such as a chapter of a book, should be placed inside quotation marks.

> *Examples:* According to Nikita Khrushchev, "Politicians are the same all over. They promise to build a bridge even where there is no river."
> His "financial forecasting tools" included a dartboard and a pair of dice.
> Their article "The Mars Effect" appeared in the July 1982 issue of *Psychology Today.*

When punctuating in conjunction with quotation marks, follow the American style (rather than the British) and place periods and commas inside the quotation marks, semicolons and colons outside. Place question marks and exclamation marks inside the quotation marks only when they are part of the quotation.

> *Examples:* "I would swap a whole cartload of precedents any time," Luther Burbank said, "for one brand new idea."
> "To what do I owe the dubious pleasure of your company?" she asked.
> "Some people exclaim, 'Give me no anecdotes of an author, but give me his works'; and yet I have often found that the anecdotes are more interesting than the works."   —Benjamin Disraeli

Semicolon

Use the semicolon between closely related independent clauses in the same sentence or when you want a break stronger than a comma but not as strong as a period.

> *Example:* "The brain is a wonderful organ; it starts working the moment you get up in the morning and doesn't stop until you get into the office."
> —Robert Lee Frost

Use the semicolon in sentences in which you already have an abundance of commas.

Example: We emphasized our local capability, low fees, and prompt delivery; and we promised personal attention, quality service, and cooperative marketing support.

Notes

CHAPTER 1

1. "Sesame Street" is an educational program for children produced by the Public Broadcasting System.
2. *Human Resources Management* magazine, cited in the August 13, 1982, edition of the Chicago *Sun-Times*.
3. *Star Wars* is the title of the 20th Century-Fox movie that revolutionized the industry with its special effects. Copyright 1977, 20th Century-Fox Film Corp.
4. John Fielden, "What Do You Mean I Can't Write?" *Harvard Business Review*, May–June 1964.
5. Bob Greene's column, the *Chicago Tribune*, June 9, 1981.

CHAPTER 2

1. Janet G. Venolia, *Write Right!* (Woodland Hills, CA: Periwinkle Press, 1980).
2. *Webster's Third New International Dictionary* (Springfield, MA: G&C Merriam Company, 1971), p. 1545.
3. *Webster's*, p. 2542.
4. John C. Hodges and Mary E. Whitten, *Harbrace College Handbook* (New York: Harcourt Brace Jovanovich, Inc., 1977), p. 281.

CHAPTER 3

1. William C. Paxson, *The Business Writing Handbook* (New York: Bantam Books, Inc., 1981), p. 3.

2. *The Writer's Resource Guide* (Cincinnati: Writer's Digest Books).
3. Charles F. Phillips and Delbert J. Duncan, *Marketing Principles and Methods* (Homewood, IL: Richard D. Irwin, Inc.), p. 543–544.

CHAPTER 4

1. Frederick C. Dyer, *Executive's Guide to Effective Reading and Speaking* (Englewood Cliffs, NJ: Prentice-Hall, Inc., 1962), p. 112.
2. *The Hemingway Reader*, Foreword by Charles Poore (New York: Charles Scribner's Sons, 1953), p. xiv.
3. Jack Trout and Al Ries, "The Positioning Era," *Advertising Age* (Chicago: Crain Communications, 1972), April 24, May 1, and May 8 issues.
4. Cleanth Brooks and Robert Penn Warren, *Fundamentals of Good Writing* (New York: Harcourt, Brace & World, Inc., 1950), p. 486–494.
5. William Strunk, Jr., and E. B. White, *The Elements of Style* (New York: Macmillan Publishing Co., Inc., 1972), p. 59.
6. Brooks and Warren, p. 458.

CHAPTER 5

1. Robert Gunning, *The Technique of Clear Writing* (New York: McGraw-Hill, 1968).
2. G. H. McLaughlin, "Smog Grading—A New Readability Formula," *Journal of Reading 12*, p. 639–646, cited by Carolyn J. Mullins, *Complete Writing Guide to Preparing Reports, Proposals, Memos, Etc.* (Englewood Cliffs, NJ: Prentice-Hall, Inc., 1980).
3. Rudolph Flesch, *How to Write, Speak and Think More Effectively,* cited by Frederick C. Dyer, *Executive's Guide to Effective Speaking and Writing* (Englewood Cliffs, NJ: Prentice-Hall, Inc., 1962), p. 201–202.
4. "STAR General Motors Computerized Simple Test Approach for Readability" (Detroit: General Motors Public Relations Staff).
5. *Style Manual,* Revised edition (Washington, DC: U. S. Government Printing Office, 1973).

6. *A Manual of Style,* 12th edition, Revised (Chicago: The University of Chicago Press, 1969).
7. *Words into Type,* 3rd edition (Englewood Cliffs, NJ: Prentice-Hall, Inc., 1974).

CHAPTER 6

1. Trout and Ries.
2. Kenneth McFarland, "The Lamplighters," a speech to the National Sales Executives Club (Grand Rapids, MI: Edward F. Miller and Associates, Inc., 1961).
3. Lewis Mumford, cited by Stewart Harral, *The Feature Writer's Handbook* (Norman: University of Oklahoma Press, 1958), p. 4.
4. Harral, p. 3.
5. Jacob M. Braude, *Braude's Treasury of Wit and Humor* (Englewood Cliffs, NJ: Prentice-Hall, Inc., 1964).
6. Richard H. Stanzfield, *Advertising Manager's Handbook* (Chicago: The Dartnell Corporation, 1970), p. 1320.

CHAPTER 15

1. Raymond V. Lesikar, *How to Write a Report Your Boss Will Read and Remember* (Homewood, IL: Dow Jones–Irwin, 1974), p. 163.
2. Paxson, p. 256.

Bibliography

Brooks, Cleanth, and Robert Penn Warren. *Fundamentals of Good Writing.* New York: Harcourt, Brace & World, Inc., 1950.

Brown, Leland. *Effective Business Report Writing,* Third Edition, Englewood Cliffs, NJ: Prentice-Hall, Inc., 1973.

Dyer, Frederick C. *Executive's Guide to Effective Writing and Speaking.* Englewood Cliffs, NJ: Prentice-Hall, Inc., 1962.

Ewing, David W. *Writing for Results in Business, Government & the Professions.* New York: John Wiley & Sons, 1974.

Hodges, John C., and Mary E. Whitten. *Harbrace College Handbook.* New York: Harcourt Brace Jovanovich, Inc., 1977.

International Dictionary of Thoughts, The, Chicago: J. G. Ferguson Publishing Company, 1969.

Lesikar, Raymond V. *How to Write a Report Your Boss Will Read and Remember.* Homewood, IL: Dow Jones–Irwin, 1974.

Mager, N. H., and S. K. Mager. *Encyclopedic Dictionary of English Usage.* Englewood Cliffs, NJ: Prentice-Hall, Inc., 1974.

Mullins, Carolyn J. *Complete Writing Guide to Preparing Reports, Proposals, Memos, Etc.* Englewood Cliffs, NJ: Prentice-Hall, Inc., 1980.

Paxson, William C. *The Business Writing Handbook.* New York: Bantam Books, Inc., 1981.

Perrin, Porter G. *Writer's Guide and Index to English.* Chicago: Scott Foresman and Company, 1950.

Phillips, Charles F., and Delbert J. Duncan. *Marketing Principles and Methods.* Homewood, IL: Richard D. Irwin, Inc., 1964.

Strunk, William, Jr., and E.B. White. *The Elements of Style*. New York: Macmillan Publishing Co., Inc., 1972.

Turabian, Kate L. *A Manual for Writers of Term Papers, Theses, and Dissertations*. Chicago: University of Chicago Press, 1967.

Venolia, Janet G. *Write Right!*, Woodland Hills, CA: Periwinkle Press, 1980.

Index

303